INTRODUCTION TO TRAINING

Penny Hackett

Penny Hackett is chief executive of Eastleigh College and has many years' experience of personnel and training as a practitioner, lecturer, and consultant. She is the author of a number of books and articles, including *Success in Managing People*; *Interview Skills Training: Practice packs for trainers*; *Choosing the Players*; and *The Selection Interview*, these last three all published by the Institute of Personnel and Development.

The only route to a professional career in personnel and development is through the achievement of the IPD's Professional Standards. The TRAINING ESSENTIALS series targets two parts of the process: Core Personnel and Development; and the four generalist modules in Employee Resourcing, Reward, Relations and Development (or their N/SVQ Level 4 equivalent). Whether you are seeking to qualify through college-based study, flexible learning or competence assessment, these texts will provide both the essential underpinning knowledge and a comprehensive framework for learning.

Other titles in the series include:

Cultivating Self-development David Megginson and Vivien Whitaker

Delivering Training Suzy Siddons

Designing Training Alison Hardingham

Developing Learning Materials Jacqui Gough

Evaluating Training Peter Bramley

Identifying Training Needs Tom Boydell and Malcolm Leary

The Institute of Personnel and Development is the leading publisher of books and reports for personnel and training professionals and students and for all those concerned with the effective management and development of people at work. For full details of all our titles please telephone the Publishing Department on 0181 263 3387.

TRAINING ESSENTIALS

INTRODUCTION TO TRAINING

Penny Hackett

INSTITUTE OF PERSONNEL AND DEVELOPMENT

Design and typesetting by Paperweight
Printed in Great Britain by
The Cromwell Press, Wiltshire

British Library Cataloguing in Publication Data
A catalogue record for this book is available from the
British Library

ISBN
0-85292-633-2

i𝕡

INSTITUTE OF PERSONNEL
AND DEVELOPMENT

IPD House, Camp Road, London SW19 4UX
Tel.: 0181 971 9000   Fax: 0181 263 3333
Registered office as above. Registered Charity No. 1038333.
A company limited by guarantee. Registered in England No. 2931892.

Contents

Introduction

This book, which introduces the IPD *Training Essentials* series, provides a general overview of the broad range of processes and activities which are part of the training function. The field is a wide and rapidly evolving one and in a text of this length we can give only a taste of what is involved. The other books in the series will take you into greater depth in specialist areas.

The aim is to provide a sound basis for understanding the role of the trainer in the context of the wider organisation. This book is intended primarily for

■ those who are already working as trainers – either in an established training department within an organisation or for a specialist training provider – and who want to get a better grasp of the function as a whole

■ those who are or aspire to be managers, supervisors and team leaders, who recognise the importance of the 'line manager as trainer' and want to learn how better to fulfil this aspect of their role

■ those who are studying training as a specialist subject or as part of a wider management programme and need a quick overview of the issues to get them started.

To help you relate the contents to your own organisation, specific tasks are included in each chapter.

These are identified like this, and may involve you in some active research or discussion with colleagues.

Each chapter ends with a summary of key learning points. Guidance on where to seek further information on particular topics is given in Chapter 11.

1

What is Training?

Introduction

Most of us have, at some time, been a 'trainer'. As the dictionary definition of training confirms, people, animals, even plants, can be 'brought to a desired standard of efficiency, condition or behaviour by instruction and practice'. Whether you have helped a colleague to master a particular work routine or a puppy to conform to acceptable standards of domestic behaviour,

> whenever you have been involved in changing behaviour, you have been a trainer.

Within most work organisations the task of bringing people to the desired standard of efficiency – or helping them to learn to do things the way they need to be done – is shared. In some, *every* employee is expected to help – by training others or themselves. In others, just team leaders, supervisors or managers may be explicitly involved. Some aspects may be dealt with by a separate training department, particularly in larger organisations. In others, training may be combined with the work of a more general personnel team. In yet others, it will fall to someone with specific technical responsibilities such as the chief engineer or to someone in another role who happens to have a particular interest in training. For a growing number, some or all aspects of training are 'outsourced' to external training providers.

Towards the end of this chapter we will look in more detail at some of the main options. Here it is enough for us to recognise that, in a business context, training can be divided into a number of different elements. Each, as we shall see, may be carried out at several levels, in different ways and at different stages in the employment relationship. These elements are:

∎ identifying training needs – in the light of the overall objectives of the organisation and the specific requirements of individuals

∎ designing and delivering training to meet those needs

∎ planning, organising, recording and monitoring the training that takes place

∎ evaluating the effectiveness of training.

Work to these four ends lies at the core of the training function – whether that is carried out by one person or a thousand, in one department or many. That it must be carried out by *someone* is beyond dispute. Wherever you look – in sports, the arts or at work – you can see the difference that training makes. The innate abilities of each member of the team, fostered and developed by effective coaching and focused on the achievement of a common goal, provide real competitive advantage. From time to time an untrained natural talent may break through and seem to disprove this. But enduring success is not based on one-off bursts of brilliance. It depends on

∎ sustained,

∎ co-ordinated,

∎ focused effort.

This is one of the things effective training can help to generate.

In later chapters we shall look more closely at each of the four elements and examine who, inside and outside the organisation, may be involved. First we shall focus briefly on some of the broader issues that help to shape the way trainers think and work. We shall consider

■ education, training and development
■ alternative training philosophies
■ national training policy
■ teaching and learning
■ organisation training policy
■ the role of 'manager as trainer'.

Education, training and development

The distinction between education and training used to be a good deal greater than it is now. Training was particular to each type of work. Education was seen as a more broadly based 'training for life'. Training was a means of ensuring specific tasks were carried out in accordance with a predetermined procedure. Education was intended to open people's minds to enable them to work from first principles and question predetermined procedures.

These distinctions have become blurred as result of changes – in both education and training.

■ Parts of the education system have become much more vocationally oriented. The General National Vocational Qualification (GNVQ) is a good example.
■ The need for constant learning and continuous improvement in ways of working within organisations has led many to encourage employees to 'learn to learn' through a much more broadly based approach to training.

Similarly, historical differences between training and development are less relevant than they were. 'Development' used to be reserved for managers or those with management potential. Management development programmes sought to equip people with the knowledge and skills they might need later in their careers, at higher levels in the organisation. This gave them a rather different flavour from the short-term, current-job focus of most training activities.

The flattening of the structure in many organisations has meant, for most, a sharp reduction in the number of rungs on the career ladder. Those roles that remain tend to be broader and require a wider range of skills than they once did. There has at the same time been a general move to empower more employees to think for themselves how best to improve the way they work. These factors combine to mean that many more people now need the chance to develop and grow, a situation once reserved for the high-flyers.

> Count the number of layers from chief executive to shop floor in your organisation today.
>
> Find someone who has been there more than 10 years and ask them how many there were when *they* started work.

Where once universities and colleges might have focused on providing education, specialist management consultants offered management development, and job-related training might have been done by technical specialists, or in house (or not at all), all three providers may now deliver elements of education, training and development.

For the trainer today the question is not so much 'is this education, or training, or development?' as 'when is this learning needed and who is best equipped to provide it?'

Teaching and learning

If some of the distinctions between education, training and development are becoming obsolete, the distinction between teaching and learning is more important than ever. *Teaching* is something one person does to another. *Learning* is something we can only do for ourselves.

Teaching may involve:

- telling
- explaining
- demonstrating
- discussing – and many other elements you probably associate with learning.

Learning

happens only when the person under instruction

- grasps the subject, mentally or physically
- translates it into words or actions that make sense to them
- locates it alongside all the other things they know or can do and
- does something with their new-found knowledge to make it their own.

The process through which this happens is known as the learning cycle – see Figure 1 on page 6.

Different people learn in different ways. They enter and leave the cycle at different points. But unless they work *around* the cycle to combine deed and thought (action and reflection), abstract and concrete (theory and test) their learning will not be complete.

This distinction is important. If training is to be of any use it has to be about helping people to learn rather than trying to teach. Not all organisations recognise this as clearly as they might, but for anyone aspiring to work in the training function it must be rule number one.

Figure 1

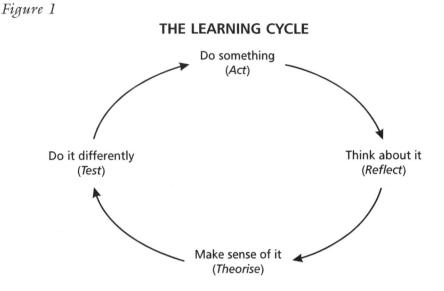

THE LEARNING CYCLE

Do something
(*Act*)

Think about it
(*Reflect*)

Make sense of it
(*Theorise*)

Do it differently
(*Test*)

Alternative philosophies

Not all organisations approach training in the same way. They vary in

■ the amount of time, money and effort devoted to it
■ the way they organise the training function
■ the relative emphasis given to different categories of employee
■ the relative emphasis given to different aspects and types of training.

Many factors have a bearing – from the size, complexity and financial position of the business to the stability of the workforce and the range and pace of change in the skills required. Perhaps more fundamental than any of these are the basic beliefs that management holds about

■ the people who make up their workforce
■ the nature of the contribution they can make.

Two brief case-studies will illustrate the point.

Company A works on the basis that if every employee carries out the tasks expected of them, to the standard that is required, the business will achieve its objectives. Its management believes that people work best when they are told exactly what to do and are closely supervised to make sure they do it.

Every new recruit, regardless of previous experience, spends time at the company training school learning how to carry out procedures relevant to their particular role. Trained instructors provide structured input and keep a watchful eye on progress. Trainees are discouraged from experimenting or asking too many questions. They are expected to learn enough to meet the standard and no more. There are tests and examinations at the end of the specified training period. Those who succeed are pronounced competent and take up their roles. Those who fail may be given a short period of remedial instruction if circumstances warrant it. If they fail again they are fired.

Once qualified for their role, successful recruits are unlikely to encounter the training function again unless – as occasionally happens – they are moved to another job requiring them to operate significantly different procedures. Otherwise 'doing as you're told' and 'not rocking the boat' are the behaviours most valued by company A.

Company B works on the basis that every employee can contribute to the success of the business in a variety of ways. Each must be able not only to do the job but also to improve it. People are selected for their ability to learn as well as for their specific job-related skills and knowledge. An individual programme of on- and off-job learning is worked out between each new employee and his or her manager – to complement existing skills and to broaden understanding of the business as a whole.

The pace and methods used are geared to the individual. There are specific milestones during the programme and regular meetings to review progress and redirect the style or content.

Once initial training is complete, a further programme is developed – with them as with all existing employees. Even if some elements have no direct bearing on the present job, this is not necessarily a problem. Learning to learn, to think laterally, ask questions and find new and better ways of doing things – these are the behaviours most highly prized by Company B.

These fictitious organisations differ in several ways:

■ Company A has what we may call an organisation-centred philosophy.

■ Company B is employee-centred.

■ Company A believes in instruction. Company B believes in coaching.

■ Company A believes in standardisation. Company B believes in individuality.

■ Company A believes in 'satisficing' – just enough training to stop people making mistakes. Company B believes in maximising – ongoing training to enable everyone, and the company, to develop and grow. In some respects, Company B could be described as a learning organisation. We shall explore this concept more fully in Chapter 10.

Neither is right or wrong; but a trainer at work in Company A is likely to experience the function rather differently from his or her counterpart in Company B.

> Which of these two companies more closely resembles the one you currently work in?

Differences in philosophy may be reflected in the way core activities such as

∎ identifying needs
∎ designing and delivering
∎ planning and recording
∎ evaluating effectiveness

are carried out. It will also be reflected in the organisation's training policy.

Organisation training policy

A policy is a framework for decision-making. It is usually established by top management – the board of directors or equivalent – to guide the decisions of other, more junior managers and employees. Table 1 highlights some of the main options when developing policies.

Table 1

POLICY CHARACTERISTICS

Either	Or
based on careful analysis of organisational needs, best practice and relevant law	intuitive
formally written down as a basis for future decisions	inferred from the pattern of decisions previously made
communicated to all employees to guide decision-making	referred to after the event to justify specific decisions
prescriptive and all-embracing	allow considerable discretion
supported by operating procedures	unsupported
part of an internally consistent framework – eg personnel policy, public relations policy	stand alone

Many contain elements from both sides of the list. Whatever your organisation's general approach, its training policy is likely to cover – explicitly or implicitly – most of the following points:

▮ the organisation's underlying philosophy/beliefs about the value of training

▮ who is eligible for training – new recruits, those recently or about to be promoted or transferred, those facing redundancy, members of designated training schemes, managers, supervisors, or all employees. (Whichever categories are included, watch out for any direct or indirect discrimination on grounds of race, sex or disability. This is illegal.)

▮ what the process is for identifying training needs – see Chapter 3

▮ what types of training are available and on what basis – job-related only, career-related, company-related or general; paid for wholly by the company, or partly or wholly at the employee's expense; conducted wholly or partly in company time or the employee's own time; supported by the purchase of relevant books, software, hardware and other relevant materials or unsupported; with or without time off for revision, exams, summer schools or field work

▮ who will decide whether a specific training proposal is covered – and to what extent

▮ what the balance should be between on- and off-job training and between the use of internal and external resources, and on what basis such decisions should be made – cost, cost-effectiveness, urgency

▮ what forms of learning/learning outcomes are favoured – self-study or IT-assisted learning or short courses, or courses leading to academic, vocational or professional qualifications, or distance learning

▮ whether employees can appeal against decisions affecting their training – and if so to whom and on what basis.

> What is your organisation's training policy?

The form and content of the policy will be determined partly by the sort of organisational factors already discussed. In addition, many organisations have started paying more attention to their training policy in the wake of some specific government initiatives. In the next section we shall consider how these shape the national training scene.

National training policy

In broad terms, government policy is to encourage the development of our national skill base through the combined efforts of employers, educational establishments and training providers, and individual employees. These efforts are co-ordinated at local level by a network of Training and Enterprise Councils (TECs) or Local Enterprise Councils (LECs) and in Scotland by Scottish Enterprise and Highlands and Islands Enterprise.

TECs are geographically based and are responsible for working to achieve national training targets in their area, as well as for delivering certain national training programmes such as Youth Training – see Chapter Seven. They can also help fund company-specific initiatives, especially if these are linked to the National Standard for Investors in People (IIP) or to the attainment of National Vocational Qualifications (NVQs) or the government's National Targets for Education and Training. To help you see how these may influence your own organisation's approach, we shall consider each in a little more detail.

National standard for Investors in People (IIP)

This is designed to raise the profile of training nation-wide by giving special recognition to those organisations which do a particularly good job of training and developing their employees. The standard is a rigorous one and requires employers to show that:

- they have a commitment to develop *all* their people to achieve business objectives
- they plan how the skills of individuals and teams are to be developed to achieve these goals
- they take action to deliver effective training for new and existing employees
- they evaluate the effectiveness of their investment in training – in terms of its effect on individuals, teams and the achievement of business objectives.

While many organisations do *some* of these things for all their employees, and others do all of them for *some* employees, relatively few are able to satisfy the IIP assessors that they do *all* of them for everyone. Some, like company A in our earlier case-study, may have decided not to try. If your company does want to, your local TEC will put you in touch with an adviser. He or she will help you gauge just how close you are to meeting all 23 elements of the standard and help you develop your training policy and processes to bring them closer to what is required. In Chapter 9 we will discuss what is involved in gaining recognition.

National Vocational Qualifications (NVQs)

In many industries and professions, traditional qualifications have now been integrated with or superseded by NVQs or Scottish Vocational Qualifications (SVQs). These qualifications, earned through on-job or continuous assessment of practical competence rather than by traditional examination, do not always require additional training. Instead they focus on raising awareness of learning that has already taken place. The candidate may be asked to produce a portfolio of examples of recent work or give a practical demonstration. Where training is needed, this can be carried out either in-house or by an external provider, so long as the subsequent assessment is carried out by a qualified assessor.

NVQs focus on competencies – that is the ability to do something – rather than just underlying theoretical knowledge or physical, mental or interpersonal skills. This sets them apart from many more traditional academic courses and, arguably, makes them more relevant to employers. Employers, through their industry and professional associations, have had a major role in the lead bodies which design the qualifications. This should further enhance their relevance.

NVQs are available at five different levels. A shop assistant or skilled factory worker may aim at level one or two initially, a supervisor at level three and senior managers at level five. Each qualification is made up of a number of units of competence. Each of these comprises specific elements of competence which are assessed against relevant performance criteria. Careful monitoring and recording of progress is essential, as is close liaison with the TEC to make the most of any funding which may be available.

Many employers have found that encouraging employees to work towards an appropriate NVQ raises self-esteem as well as enhancing skills. Some have arranged for their own managers or training instructors to qualify as assessors so that much of the work can be done in-house. A verifier, appointed by the awarding body will check periodically to make sure that standards are being maintained. NVQs are now very much part of the national training scene and many other qualifications have now been designated as 'equivalent' to a particular level.

National targets for education and training

These provide an overall framework to encourage the spread of NVQs and commitments to achieve IIP status. There are two main targets for the year 2000.

Foundation Learning

1   By age 19, 85 per cent of young people to achieve 5 GCSEs at grade C or above, an Intermediate

GNVQ or an NVQ Level 2.

2   75 per cent of young people to achieve Level 2 competence in communication, numeracy and IT by age 19; and 35 per cent to achieve Level 3 competence in these core skills by age 21.

3   By age 21, 60 per cent of young people to achieve 2 GCE A levels, an Advanced GNVQ or an NVQ Level 3.

Lifetime Learning

1   60 per cent of the workforce to be qualified to NVQ Level 3, Advanced GNVQ or 2 GCE A level standard.

2   30 per cent of the workforce to have a vocational, professional, management or academic qualification at NVQ Level 4 or above.

3   70 per cent of all organisations employing 200 or more employees, and 35 per cent of those employing 50 or more, to be recognised as Investors in People.

Other efforts to raise the profile of training take the form of national and local competitions. The most prestigious of these is the National Training Awards. Organisations and individuals who believe a particular training initiative has made a real contribution to their business performance submit details to a panel of judges. The winners receive national publicity and a trophy.

Keeping abreast of developments like these is just one of the ways in which full-time trainers can help the organisation to achieve its business objectives.

The manager as trainer

Earlier in this chapter we identified the four key elements of the training function. We have also highlighted the importance of a clear training policy and suggested some of the wider issues it may need to address. None of this presupposes the existence of training specialists. Line managers – who have direct responsibility for a particular part of the business and direct authority over the people who work for them – should see training as their responsibility too. Where this is the case, it is to the line manager as trainer that the rest of this book is addressed.

In many organisations training, or some aspects of it, is still seen as a separate activity. Table 2 on page 16 sets out some of the possible arguments for and against separating 'manager' from 'trainer'. These options are not mutually exclusive. Many organisations get the best of both worlds by training their managers to reap the advantages of 'manager as trainer', and use their own or external full-time trainers to add those which derive from the more specialist route. Others increasingly see the full-time trainer as an internal consultant, whose primary role is to work with line managers, helping them to develop the skills they need to train their own people effectively. We will explore this in Chapter 10.

Roles and responsibilities

The most logical conclusion to be drawn from Table 2 is that training responsibilities are best shared between line managers and specialists. Whether or not that is the case in your organisation will depend on how the role of personnel specialists in general and full-time trainers in particular is viewed.

▋ In some organisations, the role of the specialist may be seen purely as a service – undertaking routine work which is too time-consuming for line managers to do themselves. Keeping training records is an example.

▋ In others, the role is advisory – giving the benefit of specialist knowledge but without detracting from the line manager's right to make the key training decisions. Suggestions about training materials, methods or sources of funding come into this category.

Table 2

THE MANAGER AS TRAINER VERSUS DEDICATED TRAINERS

Manager as trainer	Dedicated trainer
Advantages	*Advantages*
∎ best placed to identify needs	∎ specialist knowledge of eg learning theory and techniques, learning resources, external providers, funding
∎ day-to-day contact – ongoing opportunities for learning	
∎ possibly better technical knowledge	∎ co-ordinated administration eg groups with shared needs can learn together cost-effectively
∎ training/coaching can become a normal part of work	
∎ full understanding of trainees' roles and responsibilities means more rounded learning	∎ better negotiating position with external providers; easier to draw together full picture of company needs; one focal point for external liaison
∎ real examples/problems provide effective basis for learning	
	∎ common learning/themes for company-wide programmes
Disadvantages	*Disadvantages*
∎ lack of specialist training knowledge, eg best practice, learning research	∎ training may be divorced from reality
∎ resources available	∎ training must usually be done in pre-scheduled doses
∎ pressure of day-to-day work may restrict time allocated	∎ trainer may have only partial knowledge
∎ planning, organising, monitoring and recording may not be best use of manager's time	∎ trainer may still need line managers' technical input
∎ managers vary in competence and commitment	∎ learning may cease when training ends
∎ harder to ensure consistent messages across the business	∎ line management involvement still essential – to identify needs, assess effectiveness
∎ may be hard to get enough distance physically and mentally between current problems and general principles	
∎ training may still have to be done away from the job – to preserve safety, customer care, and employee relationships until trainee is competent	

∎ Occasionally an audit role, checking that managers have complied with company policy, may be appropriate. Policing the performance appraisal system is an example.

∎ For some aspects executive authority may be vested in the training manager. This may be the case where the organisation's training budget is held centrally and the training manager has authority, in accordance with agreed policy and criteria, to determine how to allocate resources (see Chapter 3).

∎ Where the dedicated trainer takes on the role of internal consultant, he or she may be viewed by line managers as a fellow professional – proactively seeking out opportunities to make learning a way of life for all employees.

Whichever label best describes the nature of the relationship with line managers, there are still internal relationships within the training function to consider. Someone must develop the overall policy. Someone must plan how best to implement it, devising appropriate processes for identifying training needs, organising learning, monitoring effectiveness and so forth. Someone must put the plans into operation, using the defined procedures to achieve the planned objectives. And someone must carry out the clerical procedures needed to keep accurate information about training numbers, costs, dates and a range of other items we shall consider in Chapter 2.

In some cases the same 'someone' will perform at several different levels. In others, responsibility will be divided hierarchically. Then, too, there is scope for specialisation within the function itself. In large organisations some trainers may focus on particular business units or divisions – for example, sales or production. In others, subject specialisation may occur. One person may be an expert on finance, another on employee relations, for example.

Yet a third option is a geographical split, one person for

the north, one for the south perhaps or, if employee numbers warrant, one per site. In some organisations specialisation is by employee category – management training, technical training, clerical training and so on. Others have a combination of two or more of these approaches.

> How would you define your own role in training?
>
> Are you a dedicated trainer or a 'manager as trainer'?
>
> Do you provide a service, act as adviser, audit the activities of others, take executive responsibility or work as an internal consultant?
>
> How proactive are you in your role?

In training, as in personnel, there is no one answer. The key to an effective organisational structure will usually lie in working out what goals the function is aiming to achieve and designing a structure to fit. However roles and responsibilities within the function are to be arranged, it will not operate effectively without good initial organisation and a sound information base. These will be our focus in Chapter 2.

In brief

In this chapter we have tried to provide a general overview of what training is about. In particular we have

▌ defined training as 'activities designed to change behaviour'

▌ summarised the key elements of the training process (identifying needs, designing and delivering, planning and monitoring and evaluating effectiveness). Later chapters will explain these more fully, and the other texts in this series provide in-depth guidance on the key areas

- distinguished between education (general, knowledge-based, preparation for life) training (specific, job-related, designed to develop competence) and development (to enable people to fulfil their potential) – while recognising that these distinctions are often blurred
- highlighted the importance of the distinction between teaching (which we do to others) and learning (which we do for ourselves)
- introduced the concept of the learning cycle (act, reflect, theorise, test) and the importance of working around it to ensure learning is internalised and embedded in behaviour.

We have also looked briefly at the context in which the trainer operates – highlighting some alternative philosophies and considering some of the issues to be covered by an organisation's training policy. We gave a brief overview of national training policy, and in particular *Investors in People*, *National Vocational Qualifications*, and the *National Targets for Foundation Learning and Lifetime Learning*.

We have *not* assumed that the trainer will always be an internal specialist dedicated to the task of training, recognising instead the important and increasing role that line managers and external sources have to play in helping employees learn. Some of the advantages and disadvantages of each approach are summarised in Table 2. Later chapters will be addressed 'to whom it may concern' – that is, whoever has responsibility for the particular aspect under discussion.

Getting Organised

Introduction

This chapter is not only for those who will be working as part of a new or established training department. If you have, or aspire to, the role of line manager as trainer it will help you to understand how to approach this in an organised way, and why collecting, storing and retrieving information is so important. In it we will cover:

- setting up a training function
- setting up an information system
- training information
- sources of information.

Setting up the training function

If you are involved in setting up or formalising the training function, it is important to be clear, from the outset,

- exactly what is expected of you
- what resources you have.

If you are working on the assumption that you have a policy-making, internal consultant role while everyone else thinks you are there as a service to provide administrative support, you will be doomed to frustration. If, on the other hand, you see your role as purely administrative when senior managers are looking for proactive input to the development of training policy, your career prospects could be bleak.

Much may depend on the reasons for establishing the function in the first place. The organisation may always have invested in training its people – but in an *ad hoc* uncoordinated manner without a clear link to the corporate business plan or a coherent strategy for delivering it. In that case, creating an effective, non-bureaucratic framework for existing activity may be all that is needed.

If, on the other hand, learning has previously been through unstructured trial and error on the job, establishing the training function could demand a fundamental change of culture for everyone.

Try to get a feel for the size of the task you are being asked to undertake. Establish such basic facts as

∎ how many employees are involved
∎ what categories of employee are involved
∎ what the approach to training has been for each category
∎ what has prompted the chief executive or other decision-makers to establish the function *now*. Is it in response to:

☐ a specific one-off failure/mistake?
☐ the continuing trend in business results?
☐ 'flavour of the month' in the media?
☐ customers requesting it as part of an approach to Total Quality Management?
☐ a general drive for quality, perhaps in pursuit of industrial quality standards such as ISO 9000?
☐ a desire for recognition as an Investor in People (see Chapter 1)?

continued on page 22

continued from page 21

▌ how deeply held and widely shared the belief in training is. (Where the whole management team is eager for change your task will be different [and easier] than where doubt and back-sliding is the order of the day.)

The answers to questions like these will help to shape your role. The role which you agree initially will not necessarily be permanent. An early emphasis on administration may change to something more proactive as your contribution is established and the organisation (and you) develop. Conversely, the trainer who has internal consultancy status to begin with may find the role diminishing over time. This could be because managers are dissatisfied with the quality of your input – or because other functions have begun to seize the initiative.

Your role, and the range and level of activities in which you are expected to become involved, will determine the resources you will need. If you can, negotiate some time to assess exactly what you will require and a chance to review this after, say, six months.

Try to strike a balance when negotiating resources. You will not gain credibility by empire building. But if you stretch yourself and your people too tightly, something will snap. It is impossible to set down targets for the ratio of trainers to trainees. So much depends on the nature of the role, your starting point and the stability of the environment in which you are working. In industries with high labour turnover, or particularly complex or dangerous work processes, relatively more resources will be needed per employee.

Start by listing all the activities in which you expect to be involved. Break down each into its component parts and work out roughly

▌ how long each part takes

▌ how often it will be repeated.

If, for example, you will be involved in providing induction training for new employees – see Chapter 7 – you could work out how often there are new recruits and hence the number of courses that are likely to be needed. (There may, of course, be a trade-off between the need to induct everyone in all aspects from day one and the possibility of working with larger groups at longer intervals.) You can then calculate

$$\text{approx. no.} \times \left(\begin{array}{c} \text{time to set up} + \text{time to run} + \text{follow-up} \\ \text{each course} \qquad \text{each course} \qquad \text{time} \end{array} \right) = \begin{array}{c} \text{no. of} \\ \text{staff hours} \\ \text{required} \end{array}$$

If you can, distinguish between tasks which involve policy, planning, operational activity and clerical work (see Chapter 1.) If you repeat this process for each of your areas of involvement you will begin to get a broad picture of the time – and thus the number of employee hours – you will need.

Some areas of activity are much simpler to assess in these terms than others – hence the advice to negotiate a review period. Once the function is up and running it is much easier to monitor how much time is being spent on particular activities and modify your estimates accordingly.

1 Make a list of all the people available to help you in your training role. Enter their names in the appropriate column of the matrix below.
2 Complete the matrix on page 24 to indicate the type of contribution they can make.

Contribution Names	identifying needs	designing	delivering	recording	evaluating

You will find more discussion of the 'politics' of whom to involve in Alison Hardingham's book in this series – *Designing Training*.

Remember, too, that resources can comprise equipment as well as people. The more you can automate, the fewer people you will need. As we shall see in Chapter 5, technology-based learning can have an important contribution to make to the delivery of training and can save expensive time at an operational level. Simply by automating the production of the invitations, joining instructions and follow-up documentation, which we shall discuss in the next section, you can save on clerical time. Compare the cost of obtaining computer hardware and appropriate software against the salary and employment costs of additional clerical help before you decide.

Only if you get the right balance between people and equipment will you be able to provide an efficient and effective service. Providing an *efficient* service will usually mean being able to provide information and well-founded advice to management and trainees, often at short notice. The rest of this chapter is devoted to this. Providing an *effective* service is what the rest of the book is about.

Training information

Whatever your role, your credibility will be higher and your task immeasurably easier if you can provide

❚ clear, timely and accurate information to individual employees and their bosses, before, during and after training

❚ careful and relevant analysis of information as a basis for management decision-making – about individual employees, groups of employees and training overall.

The sort of questions you may be expected to answer fall into six broad categories.

Questions about training courses

When is the next team leaders' course? What time does it start? Who else is on it? What are the travel arrangements? Will I be able to come back for a key meeting on the second morning? What do I need to bring with me? Is there an exam? Whom do I tell about my special dietary requirements? When was the last time we redesigned the induction course? How long have we been running manual handling courses? How many people have been on them? What is the maximum number per course? Mark is on the health and safety course but I need to contact him urgently; how do I get hold of him? How long is the waiting list for intermediate training on Lotus 123? These and many more detailed questions will be directed at the course organiser or administrator on a regular basis. To answer them, a detailed course file will be needed.

Questions about training providers

Where is the best place for Harry to get his Portuguese up to scratch before we send him over there? My people want to get back into the habit of learning. How relevant are the courses at the local college? We'd like to sponsor one of our people on an MBA. Is the focus on international marketing stronger at Harvard or London Business

School? Are there any good videos on time management? Are there any good books about business process re-engineering? Does the course at UWE lead to a diploma or a certificate? Will they give any credit for prior learning? XYZ consultancy keep sending me details of their seminars. Have we sent anyone on them? Are they any good?

The breadth and scope of possible questions is enormous. To answer them at all you will need access to national or international training indexes or a comprehensive database. To answer them well you will need to understand more precisely the training need to be met – see Chapter 3.

Questions about individuals

Has George done the coaching module? When did Casey do part two of the statistical process control course? Who was his tutor for his project? What was Katie's score in the administration test? When was Robin trained on the control of substances hazardous to health regulations? What was John's timekeeping like during the interviewing course? When is Nadine scheduled to do her follow-up to the presentation skills course? Which of the training needs we identified at David's last appraisal have we still to find ways of meeting? Without a comprehensive delegate file you will not be able to respond.

Questions about groups of employees

How many of our managers have been trained in the equal opportunities policy? What proportion of the warehouse team are qualified to drive fork-lifts? How many of our shop floor are working towards NVQs? How many days' training did the machine shop get last year? Has everyone who operates a VDU had full training in the use of display screen equipment? How many of our team leaders need training in conflict resolution? How many new recruits receive training within one month of joining? Only by collating individual data for the relevant department or category of employee will you be able to answer these questions.

Questions about policies and procedures

Who do I have to get to authorise my enrolment for an Open University degree? How much exam leave am I entitled to? I can't spare Jennie on Wednesday afternoons but she seems to think she's entitled to half-day release to do her accountancy course. Who is right? My course tutor says we have to buy these three text books, but they will cost £75. Who pays? The college have rung me to ask where Michael is. He's supposed to be there. Whose job is it to investigate and discipline him? Justine refuses to go on the residential leadership course we've nominated her for because she has no one to look after her children. Can I force her to go?

Again, the possible questions are many and varied. To answer them you will need to refer to your organisation's training policy and be prepared to search for examples of how similar cases have been handled in the past.

Questions about costs and benefits

How much did we spend, per employee, last year on training? Is that more or less than the year before? Which departments spend most on training – per employee and overall? How many training course places were left unfilled this year? How many of our people have been promoted within six months of attending a personal development course? What proportion of our management trainees leave within 12 months of completing the programme? What value can we put on the changes we have made since we introduced the new 'design for innovation' course? How does that compare with the cost of the courses? What does it really cost us to put someone through the two-year technical training programme? Would it be cheaper to disband our central training team and rely on external providers? What is the correlation between the increases in our training expenditure over the last five years and the improvements in our return on sales?

Some of the information to answer questions like these may be drawn from the course and individual data mentioned above. Accurate information about costs and benefits may be harder to get. While the costs of external courses are easy to record, apportioning internal trainer time is less straightforward. Costing trainees' time, travelling costs and other expenditure may require help from the accounts department. Putting a precise cash value on the benefits can be hardest of all – as we shall see in Chapter 9.

Anticipating the sort of questions that may be asked will involve:

■ talking to line management, to establish what they feel they *must* know, under each of the six headings we have discussed. If resources permit, you can also invite them to identify what they would *like* to know on a regular basis.

■ identifying the kind of questions that may come from outside the organisation. The Health and Safety Inspectorate, the Equal Opportunities Commission and the Commission for Racial Equality are just some of the official bodies that may ask for general information from time to time. An accident or complaint could trigger a specific enquiry.

■ talking to other members of the training team to establish what questions they have been asked in the past and to agree what sort of information you should be in a position to supply.

Set yourself up a log-book or diary to record, each day, any requests for information which you have not been able to provide.

If appropriate, see if you can persuade your colleagues to do the same.

Review this once a month to see what light it sheds on the kind of information you should be keeping.

The extent to which you are able to meet every request will depend on the depth and breadth of the database you inherit or build. The speed with which you acquire the data will depend on the human or computer-based resources (or both) that you have.

Building the database will involve

■ source documents such as performance appraisal reports or training needs analyses

■ a standard pro forma for information about training events – to record objectives, duration, number of delegates, location, costs and so forth, plus, after the event, attendance lists, delegate details and performance records

■ pro formas for evaluation of training to enable trainees and their managers to provide feedback

■ an appropriate proprietary training index or a library of training materials and course information or both.

As we shall see in the next section, a computerised database will reduce the need for paper forms by allowing authorised managers to update information directly. Line managers or individual employees can be trained to identify and record training needs as they arise. Those delivering training can be trained to input and amend information about training events as they occur.

It can be more difficult to keep track of employees themselves. James White may have been a team leader in the warehouse when his last training needs analysis form was completed. If he is now a supervisor in transport you need some way of checking that this is the same James White and that his training needs, activities and costs are recorded against the right department. The closer the links between the training and personnel information systems (see below) the less of a problem this is likely to be.

'Data subjects', the people about whom computerised information is stored, have certain rights under the Data Protection Act 1984. These include the right to inspect the data held, and the right to expect that it will be used only for authorised purposes. If you intend setting up a computer-based system, or using a personnel system for training purposes, you will need to register with the Data Protection Registrar.

Everyone involved in training must of course recognise the sensitivity of some of the information to which they have access. Though training needs are nothing to be ashamed of, some employees are embarrassed that they are not yet fully competent. Even if the prevailing culture is more positive, information about who needs or has had training should only be released on a 'need to know' basis. It must never provide fodder for canteen gossip. Files and computer records must be kept secure to prevent any unauthorised access.

Setting up an information system

In all but the very smallest organisations, training administration is likely to involve using some sort of computer-based system. In larger organisations this should ideally be one that can be networked to individual trainers and perhaps line managers. By ensuring appropriate integration with the personnel system, if there is one, it will be possible to keep track of employees' movements and costs without complex updating procedures.

If you are involved in choosing whether to run the system via stand-alone PCs or mainframe terminals, the availability of equipment is likely to be a factor. If you are buying or leasing new hardware it could be worth thinking about the other uses to which it could be put.

Provided it can be reconciled with the administrator's work schedule, why not get a machine with enough capacity to run computer-based training programmes or to link in with an interactive video player or CD-ROM drive. Even if it is only available at lunch times or in the evenings it could enable you to provide additional training to those who need it. (We shall explore the contribution of some of this technology-based training in Chapter 5.)

If you are involved in choosing software, you will need to be clear whether you need

■ a means of storing and retrieving individual items of information – ie a straight alternative to a card index or

■ a means of re-sorting and analysing data – by course, by department, by date, by employee category, and so on.

If it is the latter, you will need a training database of some sort, either developed internally or selected from the proprietary systems now available. The most sophisticated of these will not only recut and analyse your data but present it for you graphically so you can monitor trends – in costs, numbers, performance ratings, achievement of course objectives – over time. They can also assist in planning future training by enabling you to model 'what if' scenarios. What will it cost if everyone who needs project management skills goes on a three-day external course? What if we use a four-day internal one instead? What if we can afford to respond only to training needs classified as top priority? What will it cost? What needs will we fail to meet?

Even if you cannot afford, or do not need, this level of sophistication you will almost certainly want your system to be capable of producing routine documentation like course invitations, joining instructions, delegate lists, requests for pre- and post-course work and evaluation. The technology is now widely available to enable you to do all these things automatically, once course and delegate details are entered.

The capital outlay involved means that the choice of both hardware and software must be approached with care.

Sources of information

The efficient administration of training depends on the accuracy and timeliness of information flow. Mistakes in joining instructions, course bookings, follow-up or the recording of information can be costly and damage the reputation of the training function. The more comprehensive and up to date the training database the less this is likely to be a problem. If you are charged with setting up such a system, do seek specialist advice. Some useful sources are:

Establishing a database

Computer manufacturers and software houses will be happy to tell you about their products and advise on their use. If there is already a personnel administration system in place and working effectively, find out about any training add-ons that may be available.

Other employers may be prepared to give you the benefit of their experience, so always ask potential system suppliers to give you the names of other users. Talk to them and, if possible, visit them to see the system in action. The picture they paint will sometimes be rather different from the one the supplier has tried to create.

Guidance on administration

Short courses designed for those new to training administration are offered regularly by the Institute of Personnel and Development. Guardian Business Services also offer a four-day course on setting up and maintaining an appropriate administration system (see Further Reading, page 171).

Information about training providers

Course objectives, target audience, costs, venues, dates and some indication of effectiveness can be obtained by subscribing to one of a number of reputable national databases – such as Omtrac or the National Training Index. Hewlett Packards' On-Demand Information Multimedia Network for Training and Personnel Professionals, developed in conjunction with BT, is also worth investigating. Alternatively, your local TEC should have a database of local providers and can access some information from national databases.

In brief

■ The first step in setting up a training function is to be absolutely clear about the nature of your role and the resources available to you.

■ To perform effectively, you will need information to enable you to answer questions – about courses, training providers, individuals and groups of trainees, policies and procedures, costs and benefits. To answer them, you will need, as a minimum:

individual records – to include information about training needs, training received, results attained

course files – to record objectives, duration, location, attenders, costs, results

a training index – to identify potential providers, dates, location and costs.

■ By working closely with line managers and other members of the training team you should get a feel for the sort of internal questions that may arise. To enable you to respond to enquiries from official external bodies, the safest course is to establish a relationship with local representatives.

■ A computerised database will speed up the collation and analysis of data – but it must be registered with the Data Protection Registrar.

3

Developing a Training Plan

Introduction

In some organisations training is not really planned at all. It is only when it becomes obvious that Robert does not know how to use a spread-sheet, or Rachel is unhelpful to customers, that training is thought of. In these instances line managers may not have any specific budget for training. If they do, they probably spend at least some of the money on other things.

In such cases, the training that is provided is often *ad hoc* and remedial. That does not necessarily mean that Robert and Rachel will not do a better job in future. It could mean that underlying or related learning needs go unnoticed, limiting the effectiveness of the training that is done.

It could also mean that Robert will be sent on an expensive external course, to be followed by a number of other employees at different times. Had the common needs of all those employees been identified earlier, it might have been possible to reduce the cost and increase the relevance of the training by bringing someone in to run it in-house.

Even more seriously, Robert may have gone to learn one system only a few weeks before a completely new one is to be installed. Without effective planning, to tie training firmly to business objectives and plans as well as to individual needs, much time and money can be wasted.

In this chapter we shall cover

∎ types of training need
∎ budgeting for training
∎ identifying training needs
∎ roles and responsibilities.

Types of training need

It may be stating the obvious to say that not all training needs are the same. Clearly someone who needs to be better at using a spread-sheet has a different need from someone who wants to improve their customer care. Such differences in content are only the tip of the iceberg. In their book in this series, *Identifying Training Needs*, Tom Boydell and Malcolm Leary differentiate three levels of performance that can each be applied to organisations, groups or individuals. The three levels of performance are:

Level 1   Implementing – bridging the gap between present and desired performance – measured against existing standards

Level 2   Improving – to achieve continually rising standards

Level 3   Innovating – doing new and better things – to produce a step change.

Our discussion will touch on all the areas of Table 3 (on page 36) – which is taken from *Identifying Training Needs*.

Training and business planning

The first task is to make sure that the objectives of the business are clear. Do management and employees have common values and a shared vision of the future? Do they know what will make the difference between success and failure – and do they know how to measure both? Until they do, your training plan is likely to be geared more to rerunning history than to inventing the future.

The development of a corporate vision and values and the identification of key business goals is a job for top management. An experienced trainer, with well-developed facilitation skills, may be called upon to assist. Their role will be to help the chief executive plan and conduct the necessary high-level meetings. At these, the management team can pool their ideas, explore their differences and hammer out statements and objectives which all agree provide a basis for the future direction of the organisation.

Table 3

ORGANISATIONAL, GROUP AND INDIVIDUAL NEEDS AT THE THREE LEVELS OF PERFORMANCE

Area of need / Level of business benefit	Organisational	Group	Individual
I_1: Implementing – doing things well	Meeting current organisational objectives	Working together to meet existing targets and standards	Being competent at the level of existing requirements
I_2: Improving – doing things better	Setting higher objectives and reaching them	Continuous improvement teams	Having and using systematic, continuous improvement skills and processes
I_3: Innovating – doing new and better things	Changing objectives and strategies	Working across boundaries to create new relationships and new products and services	Being able to work differently and more creatively with a shared sense of purpose

The processes through which these are then shared with the rest of the business – and through which feedback is provided to top management – may or may not involve the training function. Sometimes they will be passed on, down the line, without much discussion; sometimes heads of individual divisions or departments will welcome help from a trainer.

The process in one company provides an example. One of their key business objectives was to reduce the percentage of defective units which got through to the customer – an organisational improvement goal. The operations manager called on the company trainers to:

▎ help communicate this to the workforce and seek ideas on how it could be achieved

▎ provide training for line managers to help them rethink work processes and thereby eliminate problems at source, through the use of process improvement, failsafing and problem-solving techniques

▎ train operators to help them identify where and why problems start, and what they could do to put things right – using statistical process control and problem-solving

▎ train managers and operators in new ways of working. This ranged from helping managers to develop a more 'empowering' style, to helping operators to master new methods of setting up and maintaining their equipment.

Does your organisation have a clear vision and a set of values to guide the way you behave?

If so, what are they?

Where are they recorded?

What examples can you identify of behaviour (your own or other people's) that reflects these values?

If they have *not* been publicised, what would you infer them to be? (Base this on your observation of the behaviour of top management.)

Because there are so many ways in which training can help in the achievement of business objectives, it is important that senior trainers are involved at an early stage. They can then

- question which objectives are to have highest priority over, say, the next 12 months – to help assess how training activities should be sequenced or, if resources are scarce, prioritised
- look for linkages between objectives, to establish where training should start. In our example, the 'defective' problem was the only one that related directly to output, so it probably made sense to tackle it in isolation. Had the business needed to improve productivity or upgrade the perceived value of the product at the same time, a more fundamental re-think would have been needed.

If the business objectives point towards a major change of emphasis involving a significant proportion of employees, the training plan must take account of this – before any attention is paid to group or individual training needs. Only when the overall direction is clear does it make sense to start looking in detail at the impact on particular departments.

Group needs

If, for instance, improvements in customer care are seen as vital it may be appropriate to start making changes in just one or two critical areas – such as the switchboard and customer services. Although this may not be enough to compensate for the shortcomings of the product itself or of your field representatives and service personnel, these groups may be the priority. So the next part of the planning process would entail looking in detail at the way work is done in those areas, and addressing the improvements that could be made. Specific departmental training needs would emerge from this.

Individual needs

As well as planning to meet changed business and departmental objectives, we must not lose sight of Robert and Rachel. New or existing business or departmental objectives will not be met if either of them is incapable of working to the required standards. Because the organisation is made up of a lot of people like Rachel and Robert, their individual inadequacies could put a very real brake on business success.

Here, too, the trainer's input to the plan is vital. He or she may be involved directly in the identification of training needs. More likely the task would be to set up a framework and help line managers use it.

Core competencies

From the process of business and departmental objective-setting and an analysis of individual training needs, it may be clear that there are some common elements which really are essential. Particular technical or managerial competencies are what really make the difference between your organisation and its competitors. These are your core competencies. We shall discuss other types of 'competency' in Chapter 4.

> If Sony's core competence lies in developing miniaturised technology, as in the Sony Walkman, and Honda's lies in the design and manufacture of efficient and reliable engines, what are the things that set your organisation apart from others?
>
> What processes does it perform significantly better than most?
>
> In other words, what are your organisation's core competencies?

So alongside planning to meet specific short- and medium-term objectives, it may be necessary to build in an element of 'maintenance' training – to keep your core competencies topped up and to stay ahead of your rivals.

The training plan

From these four related sources

∎ business objectives
∎ group objectives
∎ individual needs
∎ maintenance/enhancement of core competencies

the company training plan will be compiled. Its precise contents will vary according to the requirements of senior management. If it is to help them, and provide a basis for measuring the effectiveness of the training function, it should at least identify

∎ numbers to be trained
∎ competencies to be developed
∎ duration of training
∎ anticipated costs.

If your senior management recognise the importance of approaching training in a planned and systematic way, you may be involved in

∎ helping to define needs and numbers
∎ researching alternative ways of meeting them
∎ costing out the alternatives (see below)
∎ putting together a timetable of off-job events (see Chapter 5).

Budgeting for training

In organisations new to training, the costs of implementing the training plan can come as a nasty shock. Unless the budget is held centrally, it will be at the planning stage that costs are most visible. Indeed, some trainers find they need to have two or even three drafts of the plan, based on different levels of provision, before the costs line up with what the business is prepared to spend.

> How much money does your organisation budget for training?
> Who holds the training budget?

The arguments for and against centralising the budget are worth thinking about. Dividing it up between different departments makes individual heads of department accountable for their own expenditure. They are the people who must answer for their departmental results, so they should be the people who decide whether or not to go ahead with training. On the other hand, training and developing employees should benefit the organisation as a whole. Why should the head of customer care meet the whole cost of training when the sales manager will benefit from increased revenue from more loyal customers?

The outcome of such debates will depend on whether top management is convinced that they will get better value for their expenditure on training from allowing one person – probably the training manager – to oversee its allocation. Some organisations take the view that this is the best way of achieving the economies of scale that can come from centralisation. Others believe that a 'free market' approach, in which in-house training facilities operate as profit centres and compete for business with external sources, helps to safeguard quality and ensure value for money. There is no right answer, and many organisations have tried both approaches – some more than once!

Whoever is paying, they will need information during the annual budgeting cycle, if there is one, to enable them to make adequate provision.

The financial aspects of training may not be what first

drew you to the function. They are, nevertheless, crucial. Their complexity will depend on

- the volume of training
- the number of training providers used
- the basis on which internal training is costed
- whether there is a training department operating as a separate profit centre and charging other departments for its services.

Identifying training needs

As we have seen, training needs may

- emerge from business plans
- arise from departmental objectives
- relate to the maintenance of core competencies
- reflect the gap between actual and required performance.

In this section we shall concentrate on the last of these. For more detailed treatment of all four aspects, consult *Identifying Training Needs*, by Tom Boydell and Malcolm Leary, in this IPD series.

Some line managers see all performance problems as training problems and will expect you, the trainer, to provide solutions. Others will insist that their people should 'try harder' or 'show greater commitment' when it is patently obvious that there is a basic lack of vital knowledge or skill.

The trainer's job is not to usurp managers' responsibility for helping their people to meet performance standards. It is to help managers identify which problems may have training solutions and to anticipate future learning needs. This is done in different ways and at different times, depending upon the organisation and its training policy. There are several possible approaches.

Performance appraisal

Performance appraisal is the regular (six-monthly or annual) review of performance by a manager and each of his or her people. It usually centres on performance against agreed job objectives, specific competencies, performance standards or personal goals.

A written report, agreed by both parties and perhaps by a more senior manager, is usually produced and a copy given to the trainer to action the training needs identified. Alternatively, there may be a further discussion between trainer and line manager to collate departmental needs on the basis of the reviews. In some organisations, appraisals between colleagues and of bosses are also conducted. These are sometimes referred to as 360° and 180° appraisals.

Performance appraisal takes many forms and can serve several purposes. These include

∎ identifying barriers to effective performance – including lack of training, unclear objectives, poor interpersonal relationships or ineffective job design

∎ enhancing employee motivation through positive feedback

∎ identifying additional responsibilities or changes in working practices which will assist in achieving departmental goals or develop the employee or both

∎ improving communication and sharing or reinforcing the vision and values of the organisation

∎ as a basis for determining performance-related pay or promotion decisions.

> Does your organisation have a performance appraisal scheme?
>
> What are its main objectives?
>
> How often is performance supposed to be reviewed?

Depending on their primary objectives, schemes may be driven by either the training or the personnel function – or by a combination of the two. The trainer's involvement can therefore take many forms including

∎ researching the need for a system

∎ reviewing alternative methods

∎ agreeing the objectives with senior management

∎ designing the scheme – which could include consideration of the frequency, performance criteria, assessment or rating method, interview style, report format and follow-up mechanisms, all of which need close line management involvement to ensure a workable scheme

∎ training appraisers and appraisees in the objectives and use of the scheme

∎ organising the printing and dispatch of forms, perhaps with basic employee data already entered to save management time

∎ monitoring the return of forms and generally policing the system

∎ collecting data from forms or direct from line managers or personnel after the appraisal interviews

∎ collating training needs to match with possible learning opportunities

∎ producing statistics and reports on overall competence levels and training needs

∎ collating the results by job category, department, division or whatever unit is the most meaningful. This will help senior management to assess whether the scheme is being systematically and fairly applied across all parts of the organisation. If one department head is rating everyone 'excellent' and another is marking everyone 'below standard', some questions may need to be asked of both.

Although appraisal can be a powerful tool in the trainer's armoury, it can also be a difficult one to maintain in working order. If the scheme does not suit the needs of the people who must use it, it will quickly fall into disrepute. Some trainers find this frustrating.

Having spent months designing a scheme, weeks training appraisers and appraisees in its use, hours getting the forms printed and organising the administration, it can be very galling to find that managers just don't bother to return the forms. Equally galling is the realisation that some of those that have been returned have clearly been written up by the appraiser with the list of company training courses open on the desk. Unless new systems or processes are being introduced, too much uniformity of needs between established employees smacks of 'me too', rather than a careful assessment of individual needs.

Performance appraisal provides a chance for employees to help identify their own training needs in relation to their present job. It is of less value when it comes to anticipating what extra skills may be needed in the future. Because of this, some organisations now use development centres as well as, or instead of, formal appraisal.

Development centres

Sometimes referred to as assessment centres, these are designed to enable participants to demonstrate a range of personal, interpersonal, managerial and technical abilities or competencies, under the eye of trained observers. A profile is then compiled to reflect relative strengths and weaknesses, or for comparison with a predetermined job profile. From this, an individual development programme can be constructed (see Chapter 7) to help overcome the weaknesses, or further reinforce the strengths.

A development centre will usually comprise a number of different individual or group tasks or exercises, each designed to allow delegates to demonstrate one or more of the relevant competencies. They are usually conducted over one or two full days, or even longer – depending on the number of competencies to be assessed. Groups of between six and 12 participants – and nearly as many managers trained as observers/assessors could be involved.

The process may appear similar to that followed in group selection or assessment centres, but it is important not to confuse the two; their objectives and outcomes differ significantly. While development centres are designed to help plan future learning and there is no 'pass/fail' outcome, assessment centres are geared to deciding which of a group of applicants comes closest to matching the requirements of a particular job. Those deemed unsuitable should, but do not always, receive feedback to help them in future job applications.

Designing and running such activities is not a job for an amateur. If you are to get involved you will need special training. As a trainer you may be asked to

▪ identify specialist consultants who can help design the process

▪ organise training for observers to ensure they know what they are looking for and how they will recognise, record and evaluate particular types of behaviour

▪ explain the nature and purpose of the activity to line managers and other employees

▪ publicise the practice so that employees who want to be considered for further development can put themselves forward

▪ make the administrative arrangements –

   ▫ booking the venue – which may need appropriate indoor and outdoor facilities. (Contrary to what you might expect, a development centre is not a place – although some larger organisations do have a fixed base, such as a company training centre, which they use)

   ▫ scheduling the events. It may be necessary to divide

participants into groups so that some can do one exercise or task while others are engaged elsewhere. Both participants and observers will need a detailed, timed programme

☐ acquiring the necessary resources. Anything from pads and pens to mobile phones, maps and specialist outdoor equipment may be required, depending on the kind of exercises involved

☐ welcoming candidates and helping to brief them on programme details

☐ acting as link/continuity person on the day, to make sure everyone is in the right place at the right time for the right activity

▮ assist with assessment – helping to mark written elements of the programme or assess practical elements

▮ draw together observers' scores and ratings to produce an overall profile

▮ provide feedback to participants

▮ design individual training programmes to meet the needs identified

▮ collate the outcome to feed into the company training plan.

Development centres, like appraisals, are both systematic and relatively formal ways of identifying individual training needs. They also require rather a lot of time and effort to set up and administer. The next method we shall consider is somewhat less labour-intensive.

Self-assessment

This can be either formal or informal. Formal methods invite employees to rate their competency against predetermined standards at regular intervals and ask for training or help if they feel they would benefit. Informal methods leave it up to the employee to work out that perhaps some training would be useful – and leave the onus on the individual to ask for it. The response will depend on the organisation's training policy, if there is one, the attitude of the line manager and the state of the training budget.

If a formal method of self-assessment operates in your organisation, you may be involved in

■ designing an appropriate pro forma for recording and assessing competencies

■ giving advice to employees on how to complete it

■ providing a specialist service to help identify which competencies are relevant to which jobs and what the appropriate standards of performance are

■ collating completed assessments and grouping those with similar needs

■ redesigning training programmes and learning packages to cross-refer to specific competencies

■ producing statistics and reports on competency levels and training needs

■ matching identified needs with possible learning opportunities.

Direct observation

It is not always necessary to set up special exercises in order to observe competency levels. Watching someone at work can be quite illuminating. Provided the observation is objective and based on specific expected actions or behaviour, it will often be all that is required as a basis for identifying training needs.

Observation may be either open (the employee knows it is taking place) or unobtrusive (the employee does not know). If, for example, your organisation has a prescribed way of answering the telephone, you can spend some time in a busy department and listen to how many staff actually do answer in the prescribed way. Alternatively, you, or a mystery caller, could ring in from outside, posing as a customer, and see what response you get.

Sometimes training needs will be identified directly through the observations of the line manager responsible. Sometimes he or she may feel it would be helpful for a trained observer to bring an objective eye to bear. Your involvement could be

▌ as an observer

▌ as the recipient of the line manager's observations.

Either way, you will need a framework against which to analyse the observations so you can assess where the real training needs lie.

Other methods

These are by no means the only ways of identifying training needs. You can

▌ undertake a content analysis of documents produced by job-holders, to identify the most frequently occurring errors

▌ interview individual employees to establish which parts of the work they find most difficult or demanding

▌ interview managers to find out what they see as the most critical differences between good and poor performers

▌ interview individual managers to see which of their employees is likely to hinder the achievement of departmental goals – and what are the factors leading to the assessment.

Who is responsible for identifying your training needs?

What methods do they use?

What part do you play in identifying the needs of others in your organisation?

What part *could* you play?

Each of the methods we have outlined can be used either to

∎ identify specific needs for one individual or

∎ establish the competencies that are needed to perform effectively.

The data collected can enable comparisons to be made between employees – and against the desired standard. To ensure that appropriate conclusions are drawn, an approach known as statistical process control can be applied. You will find full details in *Identifying Training Needs*.

Roles and responsibilities

The precise allocation of responsibilities obviously varies from one organisation to another. Much will depend on the size and culture of the organisation and on the role of the training function within it. In so far as it is possible to generalise, Table 4 sets out the likely allocation of responsibilities.

Table 4

RESPONSIBILITIES FOR PLANNING

TASK	RESPONSIBILITY
setting business objectives	top management
identification of group and individual needs	either part of the ongoing dialogue between managers and their people; or personnel manager or a senior member of the training function may set up one or more of the above frameworks to help managers and employees identify needs, depending on the extent to which learning is part of the culture
developing the organisation's training plan	personnel director or the most senior representative of the training function
producing costed proposals for inclusion in the budget	personnel director or the most senior representative of the training function

Where there is a specialist training department, managers will expect

▪ clear and user-friendly documentation to help them and their people identify and record training needs

▪ a smooth and efficient system for its issue and return

▪ coaching to help them understand the real causes of sub-standard performance (see Chapter 4)

▪ advice on possible means of meeting identified needs, together with a clear indication of the costs and time involved

▪ support in setting up development centres and training in their use

▪ performance appraisal training

▪ ongoing support and encouragement to help them get the best from their people.

In brief

▪ Although some training will and should always be necessary on a 'just-in-time' basis, most should be pre-planned and budgeted for and firmly linked to the needs of the business.

▪ Some training will focus on implementation – doing things to the required standard; some will focus on improvement – doing things to new standards; and some on innovation – doing new things.

▪ Business objectives, departmental objectives, individual needs and the maintenance or enhancement of core competencies are the main drivers of the training plan.

▪ Individual and group (generic) training needs can be identified through performance appraisal, development centres, formal or informal self-assessment, direct (open or unobtrusive) observation, content analyses, and interviews.

▪ The data produced should be used to distinguish

between natural variations in performance and real training needs.

∎ The key participants in the identification of individual training needs will be line managers and individual employees, working within frameworks designed and developed with and for them by training or personnel specialists.

4 Establishing Objectives

Introduction

You have clarified your role. You understand the training needs of the organisation, the department and of individuals. You are itching to get some training off the ground. But what exactly is it that you are going to train people to do?

The answer, you may think, is obvious. Sally and her manager want her to be quicker at using 'Amipro' for word processing. Let us send her on a course to meet her needs. But which course? Unless you delve behind the general need you may teach her the wrong things. If you do that you will be wasting valuable time and money. Worse, if Sally is still not quick enough she will become demoralised or her manager disenchanted; neither bodes well for her future. What you now need is a clear and precise set of learning objectives to enable you to plan an appropriate course of action and measure the results against a proper yardstick – see Chapter 9.

Our focus in this chapter will be

■ who to consult about training needs
■ competency-based objectives
■ translating competencies into learning objectives
■ coaching to define objectives
■ roles and responsibilities.

Whom to consult about training needs

In her contribution to this series, *Designing Training*, Alison Hardingham analyses the pros and cons of consulting

▮ customers
▮ senior/top management
▮ internal customers of intended participants – ie those who use the output that they produce
▮ external customers of intended participants
▮ the intended participants themselves

all of whom have a part to play in helping to define exactly what participants should be able to do once they have successfully completed their training.

Three principles should guide your choice:

▮ consult until you are confident that there is a real need for the training and that you know what the need is
▮ consult the people who know most about the need
▮ consult the people who should be supporting the training and its outcomes, especially those who are disaffected or hostile.

Whoever you do choose to involve, your aim is the same: to clarify exactly what it is that you want Sally to be able to do after she has been trained, to what standard and at what speed. That is, what level of competence you want her to have attained.

Competency-based objectives

Competency is 'the ability to do something', or 'the possession of the knowledge and skills needed to perform a particular task to the required standard'. This ability is translated into behaviour that can be demonstrated and observed and can therefore be measured or assessed.

In recent years organisations have invested time and effort

in attempting to define the competencies they require of employees – as a basis for recruitment and selection, appraisal and reward – as well as to help identify training needs. Where an appropriate competency framework exists the task of establishing learning objectives is relatively simple. There are several types of competency; their common characteristics are summarised in Table 5.

Table 5

CHARACTERISTICS OF COMPETENCIES

Characteristic	Definition
Behaviourally anchored	Based on examples of the desired behaviour
Observable	Can be consistently and reliably assessed by trained assessors
Forward-looking	Reflect the kind of behaviour that will be relevant tomorrow – not yesterday
Discrete	Each competency label should describe a separate set of behaviours
User-friendly	Each competency label and the behaviours associated with it should be stated in simple, jargon-free language to encourage ownership

Generic competencies

The word 'generic' means 'relating to all members of a class or group'. The 'class' in question may be all the members of an organisation or occupation. Generic organisational competencies are the abilities which are valued by the organisation because they are believed to have some bearing on the overall performance of the enterprise.

One leading insurance company has identified six such competencies as a basis for managing performance throughout the business. These are: thinking, innovating, communicating and influencing, goal-orientation, showing leadership and professional ability. This particular organisation refers to these as core competencies even though they are clearly not the same sort of concepts as the core *corporate* competencies discussed in Chapter 3.

Competencies that span *all* occupations – such as numeracy, communication and IT – are also, confusingly, described as core. Because the same word is also used to describe the compulsory elements of National Vocational (and other) Qualifications – see Chapter 1 – there is considerable scope for misunderstanding!

Generic occupational competencies are usually linked to National Vocational Qualifications. These provide frameworks that span organisations to embrace the whole of an industry sector, profession or level of management. The Institute of Personnel and Development, for example, has developed a set of professional standards for those involved in personnel and training which include both the 'things members of the profession should be able to do' – ie their occupational competencies – and the knowledge and understanding which should underpin these. The combination of vocational and academic qualifications through which these standards can be met, are highlighted in Chapter 10.

Job-specific competencies

These are abilities which enable the holder of a particular job to perform effectively. They focus on how people perform particular tasks. The same competencies may, of course, be required in several different jobs.

> What competency frameworks, if any, are used in your organisation; for whom and for what purposes?

Table 6 contains some examples of competencies. Each has a label, to describe what the competency is about, a definition and a series of descriptions of behaviour or performance indicators. Other models you may come across use clusters of dimensions to provide more detailed labels and definitions of the relevant behaviour indicators.

Table 6

SAMPLE COMPETENCIES

Label	Definition	Performance Indicators
Commercial judgement	tendency to make soundly based decisions affecting the medium- and long-term future of the business	■ takes account of a range of internal and external factors in making decisions ■ evaluates risks in a disciplined way ■ takes calculated risks to seize opportunities
Teamwork	tendency to work with the team to identify objectives and work towards their achievement	■ clarifies goals, roles and responsibilities ■ values the achievements of others ■ manages conflicts and concerns positively ■ carries others with them through a range of influencing styles ■ respects and is respected by others
Communication	tendency to share information effectively with others	■ shares appropriate information openly ■ listens and responds effectively ■ maintains consistency between words and actions ■ keeps senior management informed

Translating competencies into learning objectives

At the beginning of this chapter we used Sally's need for improvement in her word processing skills as an example. We now know that what we want her to be able to do after her training is to demonstrate enhanced competency. Assuming that her organisation has defined the competency and performance indicators associated with word processing as shown in Table 7, we are now much nearer to being able to define the objectives of her training.

By adding in performance standards for each performance indicator we can define the precise goal at which Sally must aim and which her training should equip her to achieve. Our only task now is to find out which of the three levels of competence described in Table 7 is appropriate for Sally.

Table 7

COMPETENCIES AND OBJECTIVES

Competency	Definition	Performance Indicators	Performance Standard
word processing	ability to use specified word processing software to produce timely, error-free documents	word processes letters and memoranda from hand-drafted text and audio dictation	▮ without errors ▮ in accordance with the approved house style ▮ at the rate of 12 pages of text per hour
word processing	as above	word processes reports and presentation documents using imported text and graphics	▮ without errors ▮ using the most appropriate layout and typeface ▮ at the rate of 10 pages of text per hour
word processing	as above	prepares tabulations, graphs and charts to produce word-processed reports and presentation documents	▮ without errors ▮ using the most appropriate format for the data ▮ at the rate of five pages of text per hour

These do, of course, represent three rather different levels of competence. The number of functions Sally will need to master and the options of which she will need to be aware will be considerably greater in the second and third cases than in the first. To establish which comes closest to describing the required outcome you will need to ask some more penetrating questions. You will not be able to settle for a superficial 'help her to get quicker'; you need the detail.

> Do you know what the key competencies required in your job are?
>
> What are the relevant performance indicators and standards?

Pinning people down takes perseverance. Managers often find it difficult to be precise. People do not naturally take tasks apart and put them back together again. A competence observed in others, or in ourselves, is seldom analysed in that way. We just know that Gareth is not a very good driver or that Carole is a reasonable sales rep.

Sally's word processing needs are a relatively simple example. Where competencies are more complex, the learning objectives may be harder to define. If, for example, Ray's boss wants him to be a 'better manager', we could be looking at a number of things – from working with others, to getting the best from his team; and from competence in planning and allocating resources, to effective decision-making. The learning objectives we would need to define could be many and varied. Defining them all will be a time-consuming but potentially illuminating process.

Meeting the objectives is unlikely to be achieved through a single learning event. Instead, a comprehensive training programme may need to be constructed – see Chapter 7. Many of these competencies will need to be displayed in a variety of situations and applied to a variety of problems and issues. The less clearly prescribed the task, the harder it will be to pin down exactly what you need someone to be able to do. The more discretion the job-holder has, and the more different ways there are of achieving the same results, the more complex it will be.

Not all training needs revolve around competencies. Some will relate directly to the knowledge and understanding that underpins behaviour. Others will reflect the acquisition of the basic skills which underlie specific competencies. While competency-based objectives are normally expressed in terms of

> what the learner will be able to do afterwards, eg
> 'structure a training and development session'

knowledge-based objectives are more likely to be couched in terms of

> what the learner will understand and explain: eg
> 'the purpose of objectives in training and development'

Skills-based objectives are often hard to distinguish from competency-based ones. They, too, are likely to be phrased in terms of what the learner will be able to do, but the context in which he or she is expected to do it may be less specific.

> A skills-based objective for Sally in our example might be
> 'to operate a keyboard at 50 words a minute'

A further set of objectives revolves around attitudes. A person may be able to do something and have the necessary knowledge and skills to do it – but chooses not to. We all know it makes sense to adhere to safety rules. We probably have the skills to enable us to do so. But carelessness, bravado, competing priorities for time and money can all make us lax. What we need is not a lecture on obeying the rules but something to raise our awareness that our actions could mean the difference between life and death. Only by getting the objectives clear and framing them in terms of the things the learner will believe is there a chance of success.

Where individual attitudes are concerned, matters must be approached with particular sensitivity. If someone is either consciously or unconsciously not doing their best, the reasons must be understood – not least by the person themselves. It could be that they feel undervalued in their present role. If so, training could be a way of showing that they *are* valued. But it must be the right kind of training or it will have the opposite effect.

Alternatively they may already feel or be over-qualified for the job and be disinclined to make an effort – without realising that they are doing a bad job. In that case training may be quite the wrong solution. Coaching and counselling to come to terms with the situation, or help in finding a role more suited to their talents, may be a better way forward.

> Think back to the last training course you attended.
>
> What were its objectives?
>
> Did these relate to competencies, knowledge, skills, and attitudes, or a mixture?
>
> How well were they achieved?

Figure 2 draws together the different strands we have discussed and highlights how these interrelate to contribute to performance. (The two additional elements in the model: 'basic aptitude' and 'personality' tend to be inherent attributes of the individual and are not things that can readily be changed. The former includes such things as manual dexterity or numerical reasoning. The latter covers a whole spectrum of ways in which people differ from each other. As such, they fall outside the scope of our discussion about training.)

Coaching to define objectives

Your task as a trainer is to help line managers and prospective trainees be as precise as possible. A simple 'What do you want her to be able to do after the training?' is likely to get you the answer 'A better job.' Instead you need to establish

▮ what the manager and employee see as their goal – what they are trying to achieve through training

▮ what success will look like, how they will measure it

▮ where they now stand in relation to the goal – how far short of 'ten out of ten'

▮ where and when they first became aware of the gap, in what circumstances, who else was involved, what was happening, whether there were particular time constraints or financial issues, how often it has been an issue

▮ whether there are instances where it has *not* been an issue.

Figure 2

A SIMPLE PERFORMANCE MODEL

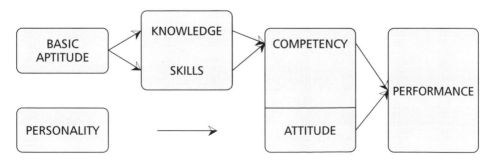

Once you have coached them through to this point, there is a possibility that the training need will disappear! There could be two reasons for this

∎ they have decided it is not worth the effort of trying to persuade you that a need exists or, more positively,

∎ the coaching process through which you have taken them will have raised their awareness of when and how the problem arises – and hence how to solve it.

The trainer who suspects that the first applies will need to probe carefully – continuing the coaching process by asking

∎ what solutions have already been tried, with what effects

∎ what options there are now

∎ how each would impact on the goal.

It may be that a solution other than formal training will emerge. If so, you will have done your job. If there is still a need for training, at least you will all by now have a very clear picture of its real objectives and can plan accordingly.

Work with a colleague to practise the sort of questions that will help you to define learning objectives.

Ask them to choose something about which they would like to know more or be better at.

Then probe to find out

∎ what they see as their goal

∎ what success will look like, how they will measure it

∎ where they now stand in relation to the goal – how far short of 'ten out of ten'

∎ where and when they first became aware of the gap, in what circumstances, who else was involved, what was happening, whether there were particular time constraints or financial issues, how often it has been an issue

∎ whether there are instances where it has *not* been an issue.

This sort of cross-examination of people whom you probably think of as your customers may not quite fit with your (or their) expectations of the training role. But, as we shall see in Chapter 10, the role of the trainer is increasingly that of internal consultant. Among other things, that means helping people to help themselves, rather than doing things for them.

Roles and responsibilities

The task of establishing learning objectives is not one that the trainer can do alone. Nevertheless, this is one area where it may be necessary to take a firm lead – and keep asking questions until you are satisfied the answers are clear enough to enable an appropriate course of action to be identified.

Depending on the organisation and its culture, you may find managers expect to deal with you direct, leaving the employee who is the subject of the conversation out of the discussion. Alternatively they may try to get you to talk to the person with the training need and be absent themselves. Neither is ideal. Workable training solutions tend to require commitment from both the employee and the manager. Far better to have an open, three-way discussion including the trainer who will deliver any off-job training which results.

In brief

- ❚ Carefully constructed learning objectives are the key to effective training.
- ❚ Objectives that are woolly or imprecise will not provide sufficient focus for the learner, nor will it be possible to evaluate precisely how well they have been achieved.
- ❚ The definition of competencies can provide a useful framework for establishing behaviourally based objectives. These are usually expressed in terms of the

things the learner will be able to do afterwards.

■ Defining objectives is easier where there are clearly defined performance indicators and standards of performance.

■ Sometimes it will be appropriate to dig a little deeper, to identify the underlying skills and knowledge that will enable competency to develop. Where this is the case, objectives will be phrased in terms of what the learner will be able to understand and explain or the basic skills he or she will be able to demonstrate.

■ The role of attitudes in learning is an important one. Sometimes it will be necessary to design training with the specific objective of changing people's beliefs about what is, or is not, appropriate behaviour.

■ The trainer's task is to consult with all those who may be able to help define learning objectives, and to coach line managers and potential learners to make sure that the objectives are clear and fully understood by all concerned.

5 Choosing Learning Methods

Introduction

It should by now be clear that there is a lot more to learning than chalk and talk in the classroom. Those with recent education in the UK will be well aware of the contribution made by group and individual project work and assignments and the role of technology as an aid to learning. Those whose memories of school or college are more distant may be surprised at the variety of methods now in use.

In Chapter 8 we shall consider how particular techniques can be incorporated into a training session. Here our focus is on the wider question of where and how learning can take place. This is a key issue for would-be trainers and training administrators to get to grips with. Specifically we will consider

- on-job versus off-job learning
- tutor-centred versus learner-centred learning
- roles and responsibilities.

The process of establishing objectives should help pinpoint the best way of meeting them. The type of awareness-raising/coaching discussion suggested in Chapter 4 can itself assist in the learning process. The choice between the options available will depend on:

- the organisation's training policy and philosophy
- the precise need to be met

- the urgency of the need
- resources (time, skills and equipment) available inside the organisation, and their location
- resources available outside the organisation
- the state of the training budget.

In broad terms the choice is between

- on-job or off-job
- tutor-centred or learner-centred.

Beyond this, there is the question of whether to use internal or external training providers. We shall return to this in Chapter 6.

On-job versus off-job learning

This question is much wider than simply the physical location of training. It affects what, how and often who is involved, as well as simply where.

On-job learning

On-job learning is not always conscious or structured. Personal reflection on what seems to work, or please the boss, or satisfy the customer, leads people to try alternatives and modify their behaviour without external support. This spontaneous movement around the learning cycle can be fostered by providing diaries or learning-logs to encourage reflection. In some organisations, self-coaching using the sort of questions discussed later in this chapter increases the benefits to be gained.

Nor is on-job learning restricted to the learner's own job. Job rotation or secondments to other parts of the organisation can broaden the opportunities for learning. Membership of task forces, working parties or special projects can provide further learning opportunities within a job.

For the purposes of this discussion we shall define on-job learning as learning that takes place in the learner's normal workplace, in the course of doing their work. For the manager as trainer, training at the desk or workbench is often the obvious solution to all training needs. For the specialist trainer, it is sometimes the last to be thought of.

The label of 'on-job' learning can cover a multitude of approaches: everything from 'sink or swim' and 'learn by your mistakes', via the traditional 'sit next to Nelly' or a more formal 'buddy system', to a carefully planned programme of on-job coaching, working through the elements of the task in logical sequence with a skilled coach. Each may have something to offer, depending on circumstances. All will benefit from being used in a planned and controlled way.

The trainer's skill lies in

▌ identifying the level of support the learner will need
▌ working out who can give it.

Sometimes it may be appropriate to let an individual or team work through a particular project or piece of work without much help – and then review the whole thing at the end to draw out and help reinforce learning. Sometimes it may be better to have someone working alongside who can provide minute-by-minute coaching and support. One of the pitfalls for the training zealot is to assume that such coaching is always necessary.

Clearly, where questions of safety are involved a novice must *never* be left alone to work out the best way of operating dangerous equipment. Elsewhere, a small amount of initial coaching, followed by review sessions at key points, can work well. In general, for learning to be effective it helps if there is careful distinction between tasks which *must* be done in a prescribed manner in order to produce the required quality or speed of output, and those where the individual is free to use his or her own initiative.

For tasks in the first category, the trainer's efforts may need to be devoted to producing a clear and logical step-by-step procedural manual so learners can familiarise themselves with the process and refer to the manual as they work.

What procedural manuals does your organisation have?

How up to date are they?

Who uses them?

What for?

How useful are they?

How could they be made more useful?

Alternatively, and potentially more effectively, someone may coach the learner from first principles. If the steps needed to complete the task are logical the learner should be able to work them out – and remember them as a result. You will need to:

- refrain from long and detailed explanations and demonstrations
- identify a logical place to start. For some tasks it is possible to allow learners to experiment – to 'find out what happens if I press this key or pull that lever'. For others it could be disastrous. Then you will do better by asking the learner to think about what the machine is designed to do, what control he or she will need over it, and so on
- observe the learner, asking questions to help raise awareness. If he or she focuses on 'what I notice when I do this', adjustments to posture, grip, tension, and so on, will follow until it feels right.

You may or may not get involved directly in this sort of on-job coaching. The person's own boss, or a colleague, may be better placed to give it. Where *you* might need to set up special sessions to go down to the employee's place of work for a period, *they* may be there already. Where *you* might need to acquaint yourself with current working practice, *they* are already aware of it. Where *you* will have to walk away at the end of the session, *they* may be able to give extra *ad hoc* coaching through the working day or beyond. On the other hand, because you do not know the detail, you will have to coach; the boss or a colleague may think it is quicker to tell. Because you do not have direct experience of the task, you will have to encourage the learner to think; the boss or a colleague will be more inclined to show how to do it – their way.

Whoever provides support for on-job learning needs to develop effective coaching and questioning skills – rather than instructing or telling. These are at least as important as competence in the task itself. Where you will need competence is in understanding when the trainee is performing to the required standard. If learning is directed towards achieving an NVQ as well as satisfactory job performance, someone must be trained to assess whether the right level of competence has been reached.

The benefits of on-job learning

▌ Training is carried out in the same circumstances as the job itself. The trainee should have no problem in seeing the relevance of what is being learned, or in transferring it back to the job.

▌ Training can more readily be provided on a just-in-time basis, exactly when needed, rather than at predetermined times.

▌ There may be less need for special equipment or materials to be provided. Depending on safety and output considerations, it may be possible to use operational resources.

Some of the key issues for anyone contemplating on-job learning are:

▌ Is the training properly planned?
▌ Will enough time and resources be devoted to it?

■ Will it be properly documented?

■ Will it be conducted by an effective coach?

■ Has proper account been taken of any health or safety hazards?

■ Will competence be assessed fairly and accurately?

■ Will it be carefully evaluated (see Chapter 9)?

> If you were promoted and someone new was appointed to replace you, which aspects of your job do you think it would be best for them to learn through on-job training?
>
> Who, apart from yourself, could give them that training?

Off-job learning

This takes many forms, depending upon the specific objectives to be met. Some methods, such as lectures, presentations and private study via books and articles, are designed to pass on knowledge. Others, such as demonstrations and role plays, are more suited to skills-based learning. Yet others, such as project work and simulations, can bring knowledge and skill together to develop competencies.

Off-job learning may be the only way to acquire the background knowledge needed for some jobs. Indeed, off-job learning, in the form of academic study or vocational training, is usually part of the employee specification for recruitment. Beyond that, it will often be necessary to make sure people know the basics, the underlying theories or legislation governing particular types of work.

It may also be the only safe way to allow learners to practise skills or develop competence without slowing output or reducing quality. It might, for instance, be risky to allow a customer service representative to practise on real customers before he or she has learnt something of the company's policy and how to demonstrate its products to best effect.

Off-job training can be carried out one-to-one by the learner's own manager or colleagues, simply using space and equipment away from the normal workplace. It can also take the form of reading or other types of private study, again on an individual basis. More usually it entails a number of employees with similar needs being brought together away from their desks or workbenches.

> If you were promoted and someone new was appointed to replace you, which aspects of your job do you think it would be best for them to learn through off-job training?
>
> Who would be best placed to provide that training?

The tasks involved in off-job training fall into three broad categories. We shall consider each in turn.

1 Resource co-ordination

This may involve:

- identifying and acquiring appropriate space for the learning to take place. This might just be a corner of the workshop or office, the canteen or, for outdoor team-building events, the car park. Alternatively it could mean researching conference centres and hotels, negotiating rates and assessing auditorium and seminar room space

- identifying and acquiring appropriate hardware. This could mean begging or borrowing a couple of PCs to set up a computer-based training resource – see below. It could mean acquiring bits of semi-obsolete or under-utilised production equipment to get people started on. It could mean hiring in, leasing or buying a video camera and VCR. In fact, depending on the training involved, it could mean anything from golf nets and tennis rackets to wet-suits, ropes and breathing apparatus. Some, but by no means all, of the equipment is likely to be found in the workplace. The increasing popularity of outdoor and activity-based training as a means of developing leadership and team skills means that tents and torches are as much part of the resource co-ordinator's stock in trade as flip charts and overhead projectors

▌ identifying and acquiring appropriate software. Books, videos, computer-based training packages, interactive video discs, CD-ROM, training packs, games, simulations, all form part of the trainer's armoury. Someone must keep up to date with the latest technical and managerial texts. Someone must trawl through the catalogues and publicity leaflets to identify relevant material. Someone must attend video previews or arrange preview hire to evaluate material. In short, someone must look at the latest training material and make the case for buying, hiring or borrowing the most relevant items.

In some organisations, these responsibilities will be shared between all those involved in training. Everyone will keep an ear to the ground and suggest, to the training manager if there is one, what may be worth getting. In others, one or more specialists may spend some or all of their time on this.

2 Administration

This in turn divides into a number of specific areas:

Resource administration

In some organisations the sort of learning resources we have been discussing are brought together in a formal library or learning resource centre. If this is big enough, it may be a full-time job cataloguing material, supervising its use or recording and monitoring loans. Sometimes usage is restricted to other trainers. Sometimes books, videos and technology-based learning packages will be available to all employees, for use at the centre, back at work or at home.

Hardware, too, may be available on loan and someone must keep track of who has borrowed it and when it is due to be returned. And someone must maintain the equipment in usable condition, checking overhead projector bulbs and the functioning of computers and video equipment. Depending on the frequency of use and the number of different users, this can be quite a responsibility. Where no one accepts that responsibility, equipment will go astray or be damaged and future trainees will find that key resources seem to have disappeared.

Course administration

In Chapter 2 we touched on some of the administrative elements involved in getting people on to courses and recording their attendance and results. Although there is an administrative element where training is done on-job, this will not usually extend beyond recording the fact that training has taken place and competence achieved. It is where there is a substantial element of off-job learning, on internal or external courses, that the administrative burden is heaviest.

To begin with, the calendar of training events must be produced – based on the organisation training plan (see Chapter 3). This may in turn require much toing and froing between in-house trainers and other providers to ensure the sequence is logical, fits with their other commitments and does not clash with other events in the company timetable or that of potential delegates. The latter can be particularly problematic. The fact that a group of employees has a common training need does not mean they will all be ready, willing and able to start tackling it on the second Monday in August. Some will be on holiday, some will be in departments that are short-staffed, some will be off sick, and so on. Even once the date has been agreed there are still many more administrative details to be tackled.

Space and other resources must be booked and, where

appropriate, prices negotiated and payment progressed. Delegates and trainers must be advised of locations, sent maps and instructions about when and where to report.

Travel arrangements for trainers and possibly for trainees may have to be made and paid for. Overnight accommodation may need to be reserved for some or all of those involved, as may coffee on arrival and mid-morning, lunch, tea, dinner, bottled water and peppermints!

Lists of those attending will need to be produced, before and after the event. Individual and departmental training records must be updated. Delegate name badges and place-names may be needed – and will have to be issued as delegates arrive – perhaps along with a delegate pack of paper, pens, programme, delegate list. Sometimes copies of handout material or course notes will also be part of the pack.

Telephone calls for those attending may have to be fielded to avoid interrupting the session – and passed on at break times. An outgoing message service may also be provided and, for large events, regular liaison with caterers or hotel staff may be needed – to adjust the air conditioning, explain how the lights work, stop the noise from the next room, etc.

3 Design of off-job training

Again, there are several facets. Just because learning will take place away from the job, this does not imply attendance at a training *course*. An increasing proportion of all our learning is now being done via technology and books and manuals. You will find detailed advice on how to develop such materials in Jacqui Gough's book in this series – *Developing Learning Materials*. Here we have space only for a brief overview.

Learning materials

A key skill for many trainers is the ability to compile and

create attractive, user-friendly materials for private study. Aspiring authors of such materials need

■ a thorough grasp of the topic

■ the ability to look at it through the eyes of the learner and pitch the language and content accordingly

■ the skill and patience to work and re-work the material, making use of illustrations, flow diagrams, self-test questions and a host of other devices all designed to involve the learner and help generate active participation rather than passive – and therefore probably ineffective – reading

■ the assertiveness to ensure that learning materials designed for novices are not vetoed by their more experienced bosses, who may want something that looks more like the pack they saw at a recent exhibition than a usable in-house tool

■ possibly, proficiency in desk-top publishing. This will enable them to play around with the layout and assess the impact of alternative presentational devices without having to hand the work over to anyone else. Alternatively, an assistant who is proficient in basic layout and design can complement the author's technical knowledge and training expertise.

Course design

Putting together a training programme is the subject of Chapter 7. Conducting a session, using a range of tools and techniques, is dealt with in Chapter 8. Here we are concerned with the sequencing of items within a learning event. You will find more detailed treatment of this in Alison Hardingham's book, *Designing Training*.

For every off-job learning event, someone must take the learning objectives and work through, in detail, the knowledge and skills that will be needed if the learner is to emerge with the required level of competence. Only then will they be able to answer the key questions listed below.

Course design questions

▌ Where should we start?

▌ How long should it take to get trainees from the start point to where they need to be?

▌ Who is the best person to help them get there?

▌ should the training be tutor-centred or learner-centred?

▌ In what order should we tackle things – are there some things which the learner will have to be able to do in order to master other elements?

▌ What learning methods are likely to be most appropriate – presentations, practical exercises, role play, case-studies?

▌ What exercises/materials do we have/can we design?

▌ What additional aids will help – videos, CD-ROM – and do we have them?

▌ Can we get them when we want them?

▌ When would it be best for the training to take place – what time of day, day of the week, weeks of the year, will strike the right balance between trainees' needs, likely attentions spans, the commercial needs of the business?

▌ What sort of venue/location would be most conducive to achieving the objectives?

Only when these questions have been answered in a manner satisfactory to trainees' bosses is the trainer ready to get the trainees together and start work.

Tutor-centred versus learner-centred training

Much of our discussion so far has taken an organisational perspective on training. We have assumed that the identification of training needs and the choice of methods of meeting them is something an employer does for – or hopefully, with – each employee. New patterns of work and the development of 'portfolio careers', combined with some of the shifts in managerial behaviour identified in Chapter 10, cast doubt on whether this assumption does, or should, always hold.

Self-development, driven by the individual employee, with or without support from the employer, has an increasingly important part to play. In their book in this series, *Cultivating Self-development*, David Megginson and Vivien Whitaker explore the implications of this and identify a range of ways of supporting self-development.

Self-development means that it is the learner who accepts overall responsibility for learning. It does not necessarily mean that only learner-centred learning methods will be used. Both tutor-centred and learner-centred training may be assisted by the use of technology – although it is in the area of learner-centred training that this really comes into its own.

> Tutor-centred training gives the tutor control over pace and content.
>
> Learner-centred training gives the learner control over pace and content.
>
> Coaching enables tutor and learner to share control.

Tutor-centred training

Lectures and presentations are the most obviously tutor-centred methods. The trainer decides the content and delivers it at the pace he or she thinks appropriate. The learners can, of course, slow things down – by asking lots of questions or misbehaving. They are less likely to be able to speed things up – at least in the short term. They do still have some choices to make – to listen or not, to ask questions or not, but the trainer sets the pace.

Role plays and practical exercises are more participative. Trainees can determine the pace a little more. But it is generally the tutor who decides which role plays or exercises to use. And it is likely to be the tutor who sets the timetable, structures the debriefing session and draws out the key learning points.

These methods suit some trainees and some learning objectives quite well. Lectures, for instance, can be a useful way of passing on factual information – especially if accompanied by demonstrations, illustrations and handouts to reinforce key messages. Role plays can give people confidence in handling unfamiliar situations and enable them to test out different approaches to dealing with customers, interviewing staff or tackling other interpersonal issues. Practical exercises can give hands-on experience of anything from constructing a menu to leading a team, and from compiling a report to planning an advertising campaign.

Learner-centred training

At the other extreme are methods which give the learner more or less complete control. At the traditional end of the spectrum lie printed books and journals and self-study texts. Self-development questionnaires, learning-logs and other tools described by David Megginson and Vivien Whitaker in *Cultivating Self-development* provide scope for more active learning. The various forms of technology-based training described in Jacqui Gough's *Developing Learning Materials* are also generally designed to be learner-centred. With computer-based training, CD-I and CD-ROM packages, the learner can usually

∎ decide when to switch on
∎ decide when to switch off
∎ fast-forward to move ahead
∎ go back to key points
∎ test out what happens when the wrong answer is given
∎ find out what happens when the right answer is given
∎ ask for help when needed.

In short, he or she has, in the more advanced packages, a completely flexible, all-knowing tutor at the touch of a key or the click of a mouse button. With CD-ROM or CD-I it is possible to check things out from a number of different angles – see the video, hear the sound-track, watch the screen, answer the questions and get truly involved with the learning process. Well designed technology based training has many advantages.

Advantages of technology-based training

■ It is stimulating and involving.

■ It takes learners right around the learning cycle.

■ It can be used time and again by the same or different employees.

■ It is quick and easy to learn to use.

This sounds like the ideal solution for many learners. It means they can follow their own interests and work at their own pace.

But for some, especially those who have never heard of CD-ROM and are afraid of mice – especially the computer kind – it sounds like a nightmare. It also has the disadvantage of being relatively expensive to produce and the range of products on offer is still limited and of variable quality. It may also leave the learner a little too free to determine the pace. Although some packages do record progress and test learning, that has a 'Big brother is watching you' connotation which makes some trainers and learners uncomfortable.

Coaching

This is the only method that really allows trainer and trainee to develop a learning partnership and to share control. We have already referred to coaching several times without fully defining it. In essence it involves

■ identifying a clear, challenging yet realistic goal or learning objective. This should be something the learner wants to achieve rather than being prescribed by the trainer – though it needs to be set in the context of the overall objectives of the training programme

■ raising awareness of where the learner currently stands in relation to the goal and of when, where, how often and in what circumstances it is an issue. The coach asks the questions. In searching for the answers the trainee learns more about the reality of how he or she is approaching the task at present and begins to identify some possible directions for change

■ identifying options – the things the learner could do to get nearer the goal. Initially all the ideas should come from the learner without any attempt to evaluate them or decide which to adopt. The trainer's ideas don't form part of the process unless the learner asks for suggestions. Only when all the learner's ideas have been listed will the coach ask the learner to begin to weigh up the possibilities, working through each option to see how it might help and what it would take to make it work; determining which action the learner will take. This will normally emerge quite spontaneously as the learner narrows down the options

■ pinning down exactly what the learner will do, by when, what help is needed, what obstacles must be overcome and how that will be done.

Because the coach is there, asking questions and listening attentively to the replies, the learner should never feel isolated or left to his or her own devices. Because the learner is totally involved in setting the goal and answering the questions, the trainer need never fear that the learner has switched off or lost interest.

Coaching can be used with teams, groups or individuals. It can also be used as a general problem-solving process. The basic principles of questioning and the model of working from the goal, through reality, to options and will, hold in all these contexts. It is therefore perhaps *the* key skill for anyone aspiring to get involved in training.

---

1 Think about all the learning methods to which you have been exposed in your life to date.
2 Enter them in the first column of the matrix below.
3 Complete the matrix to indicate whether, as you experienced them, they were essentially tutor-centred or learner-centred.

Method	Tutor-centred	Learner-centred
1		
2		
3		
4		
5		
6		
7		
8		
9		

Roles and responsibilities

On-job coaching is best done by the trainee's own boss or a colleague. Off-job training can be done by any combination of line management and internal or external training specialists competent to contribute.

In some organisations, training and resource administration are separate functions – with different people dedicated to each; in others, those responsible for delivering training are expected to handle their own administration. Much will depend on the size of the organisation and the volume and complexity of the training requirement. In most of those where there is a specialist training function, line managers are likely to expect support in

∎ choosing appropriate methods

■ planning appropriate courses, perhaps with a published timetable or calendar to suit the needs of the business

■ acquiring and evaluating training materials

■ managing the resource centre, if there is one, and keeping track of its contents

■ booking training venues and handling the associated administration

■ devising and managing a simple but effective system of course nominations and confirmations, with joining instructions sent out in good time

■ implementing proper attendance and performance records for off-job training.

Some line managers are happy to build up their own contribution to off-job as well as on-job training. Others will require encouragement or coaching, from you or their own boss, to do so.

In brief

■ Designing training involves making choices – between on- and off-job learning and between tutor- and learner-centred methods.

■ The factors that will shape these choices include the organisation's training policy, the time, money and other resources available and, of course, the learning objectives to be met.

■ Not all training is driven by the organisation; there is an increasing acceptance of the individual's responsibility, reflected in a trend towards self-development.

■ On-job learning can include participation in secondments, task forces, working parties and special projects as well as learning in the course of normal work.

■ The amount of support needed for on-job learning will vary, but considerations of safety should always be paramount.

▌ Effective coaching is the key to successful on-job learning – and can be carried out by line managers, colleagues or trainers, provided they have the necessary skills.

▌ Transfer of learning will often be greater for on-job training, and the additional physical resources required will be less than for off-job training. But planning and monitoring may be less effective and underlying knowledge and skills may be harder to develop.

▌ The administration of the resources needed to support off-job learning can be a specialist training role in its own right. It involves managing space and accommodation, hardware, software, and other learning resources, as well as the production of course documentation.

▌ Designing off-job training requires competence in designing or choosing learning materials as well as the design of the event itself.

▌ Some learning methods – such as lectures and case-studies, are essentially tutor-centred. Others, like much technology-based training are learner-centred. Coaching enables tutor and learner to work in partnership to establish

    ▢ Goal

    ▢ Reality

    ▢ Options

    ▢ Will.

6

Choosing Training Suppliers

Introduction

In some instances the choice of training provider may precede the choice of a specific method; the provider may be the best judge of how to meet the objectives. In other cases, the internal trainer will decide on the type of approach required and then select a supplier with expertise in using it.

If, for example, a team of external consultants has been appointed, their task will start with close scrutiny of the initial objectives – which may be amended in the light of the questions they raise. They will advise on the sequence of learning, the mix of on- and off-job and the specific methods to be used.

At the other extreme, if it has already been decided that there is a need to be met through some form of technology-based learning, the resource co-ordinator, or the trainer themselves, will need to search the relevant directories to identify and evaluate appropriate suppliers.

Either way, getting the right supplier can be critical to successful learning. The first choice to be made is between internal and external resources. This will be governed by the same sort of factors as we listed in Chapter 5. Here we will cover

- external sources
- internal sources

■ open versus tailored training
■ roles and responsibilities.

External sources

There is no shortage of directories and databases to help with the identification of external suppliers. A few are listed in Chapter 11. There is usually no difficulty getting your company added to the mailing lists of consultancies, business schools, or other suppliers. (You may sometimes find it harder to get it deleted!)

The trainer or resource co-ordinator needs to be able to identify and apply appropriate selection criteria. These could include a host of issues, including

■ reputation – of the supplier organisation or key members of it
■ fit with the organisation's own ethos and values
■ exclusivity (not currently working for a competitor)
■ cost
■ geographical location
■ availability at the required time.

> Make a list of some of your organisation's recent training events, indicating who provided each.
>
> Highlight those that were conducted by external providers.
>
> What do you think the criteria were for
> (a) using external suppliers rather than internal
> (b) using the particular suppliers chosen?

The overriding consideration will, of course, be proficiency in achieving the required learning objectives. You will have to choose between those who specialise in a particular area and those who offer a wider portfolio. If, for example, the need is for someone to provide telephone skills training, your choice might be between

∎ the business unit at your local college

∎ a specialist local consultant

∎ the supplier of your telephone hardware

∎ another telephone company

∎ a company specialising in communications training

∎ a company offering office and administrative training

∎ a company with a complete portfolio of managerial, administrative and clerical courses.

(We shall, for the moment, discount the possibility of interactive media.)

The process should follow the outline in Table 8 overleaf.

In many instances the process for making such decisions involves senior line managers, and possibly trainees, as well as those directly involved in the training function. You may find that setting up meetings, clarifying expectations and documenting agreements reached among the internal parties is as much a part of arranging external training as the learning itself.

As with any other selection process, the trainer must be sensitive to the candidates' needs as well as those of the organisation. For the would-be training provider, the time spent pitching for new business represents a major cost. You should not lightly ask for detailed, tailored proposals unless you are seriously considering someone.

As well as competence in using the relevant directories and databases, some of which are quite complex in their structure and the amount of detail they contain, you will need:

∎ detailed understanding of the objectives to be met

∎ some understanding of the relevant subject area so you can recognise appropriate lines of enquiry even if your own 'key words' don't appear in a particular directory

Table 8

SELECTING EXTERNAL PROVIDERS

Process	Explanation
1 *Research the options*	This could involve extensive trawling through directories and brochures, then telephone calls followed by meetings with a shortlist of possible providers or third-party sources, such as the Training and Enterprise Council, to establish their track record.
2 *Consider the wider issues*	If the proposed training is only the first step in a larger training plan it may make sense to start working with someone who will be able to contribute more later – reducing the amount of familiarisation time that will be needed before subsequent stages. Against this must be weighed the issue of trainer credibility. While familiarity will save time, having the same so-called 'specialist' popping up on six different subjects may stretch the credulity of trainees.
3 *Clarify the detail*	Just what is the provider offering to do, when, where, for how many trainees, over how long a period, at what cost, with what learning methods and with what guarantees of success?
4 *Impartially weigh up the pros and cons of each option*	Apply your selection criteria as objectively as possible.
5 *Make a decision or recommend an appropriate provider*	Which you do will depend on your role and authority, and who else is involved in decision-making.

■ cataloguing, filing and indexing skills to organise literature into a meaningful system, especially where external databases are not available

■ sound administrative skills and a good memory – to keep track of progress

■ a clear, logical and analytical approach to weigh up options

■ personal integrity – to resist the blandishments of less scrupulous providers.

Internal sources

In Chapter 5 we considered the choice between on- and off-job provision. Here the issue is which of a number of possible trainers should be nominated to help achieve particular learning objectives. The factors to be considered include:

▪ subject expertise
▪ coaching skills
▪ commitment to helping others learn
▪ competence in using relevant learning methods
▪ credibility with trainees
▪ availability – at the times and in the locations where training will take place.

Sometimes there is only one possible contender, but often you will be faced with a choice – perhaps between the 'subject expert' and the less prominent but potentially more effective 'coach'. This can put the trainer in a somewhat awkward position. A senior manager, expert in the field, takes it for granted that he or she will be giving the required input. You may know, from past experience, that

▪ the trainees will be bored stiff
▪ the content will be pitched too high
▪ a more junior member of the manager's team is much better at starting from where the learners are, seeing the subject from their perspective, and coaching them to achieve the learning objectives.

Someone will have to manage this potential conflict without damaging the attainment of those objectives, the senior manager's self-esteem or their own career prospects!

Someone will also have to keep track of which employees are competent in training others. In some organisations, 'training to train' is an accepted part of the training programme for managers and team leaders. Where NVQs are in place, at least some line managers are likely to be trained as assessors – and hence fully understand the competencies that trainees are required to master and how this will be demonstrated in their work.

In such instances, particularly in larger organisations, it is helpful to keep a register of trainers plus details of when their services are called upon. If the requirement is frequent it can save time in the long run to establish and maintain an 'availability' calendar with each of these potential trainers.

Make a list of those you would like to contribute to one of your in-house programmes. Enter their names in the appropriate column of the matrix.

Check their availability on the relevant dates and complete the matrix.

Name \ Date	Day 1	Day 2	Day 3	Day 4	Day 5

By finding out, recording and regularly updating a database showing when they are not available because of departmental deadlines, major events, peak periods or their own or other people's holidays you can save a lot of phone calls and all-round frustration.

Open versus tailored training

As we have seen, there are lots of choices to be made in training. Yet another is the choice between 'open' and 'tailored' training.

Open – or public – training is, in its purest sense, available to all-comers – ie to any company or part of a company that wishes to nominate delegates.

Tailored training is designed to meet the specific needs of a particular organisation, or part of it.

The terms are most frequently used in the context of external provision. Here truly open courses are those for which there are no entry requirements beyond the ability to find the course fee. Pre-screening of delegates is limited, although the more reputable providers will do their best to prevent any major mismatches between delegate and trainer expectations.

Open courses may be offered several times a year via brochures, mailshots, training indexes and databases. The provider will generally try to give a reasonable insight into the objectives, content, methods and target audience for the course. There is usually an upper and lower limit on the number of delegates. This can be useful to know. Too few delegates can be just as counter-productive as too many unless the learning methods are adapted accordingly. The training provider who simply reduces the amount of trainer support to keep costs down and protect profit margins is not necessarily doing your trainees any favours.

Table 9 on page 92 sets out some of the advantages and disadvantages of open courses.

The process of nominating, briefing and debriefing delegates for open training is likely to be slightly different from that for tailored or in-house training. Particularly careful evaluation is needed to help build a register of 'approved suppliers' – those courses and providers that are worth using again.

In some organisations extra monitoring processes are set up to make sure that trainees actually do attend. This may occasionally be a problem where, for instance, the employer provides day release to attend a course and the trainee unilaterally decides there are better things to do on a Wednesday afternoon. Because day release courses

Table 9

ADVANTAGES AND DISADVANTAGES OF OPEN COURSES

Advantages	Disadvantages
Trainees are exposed to people from other organisations – which can help broaden their perspective.	The presence of delegates from many different types of organisation with differing needs can be a distraction – and may occasionally lead to disenchantment with the participant's own company.
The provider may be able to pull together specialists in particular subject areas to provide a more rounded programme than would otherwise be possible.	Because learning is not company-specific, trainees, and their bosses, must critically assess which parts of the learning really fit back in the workplace.
The costs per head may be lower than for comparable tailored programmes, because development costs can be spread across several courses.	Sometimes a manager will be overly critical of the 'academic' theory learnt, dismissing it as irrelevant to the real world. Sometimes a trainee will uncritically accept that principles and practices they have been taught must apply in their entirety, without recognising the differences in objectives, structure, culture, work processes, relationships and other factors. These can mean that transplanting ideas can be just as accident prone as any other kind of transplant. Unless the ground is well prepared and the climate conducive, it may be better not to try.

generally lead to qualifications of some kind, some employers may be tolerant, and reckon that the end justifies the means. If the qualification is achieved, it is up to the trainee to decide how best to allocate his or her time. Others take a less lenient view and insist that the course provider notify them of any absence so it can be tackled immediately.

It is not only courses that can be open or tailored. The costs of developing and producing books, videos, computer-based training and interactive multi-media programmes often have to be shared between a number of people if they are to be offered at affordable prices.

While not all the advantages and disadvantages apply in the same way, the problem of applying the general principles they contain in the specific context in which trainees are working is a continuing issue. For this reason, the idea of working in partnership with one or more providers to customise an existing programme, or design one from scratch, can be attractive.

You are more likely to find tailored training in larger organisations where there are significant numbers of people with the same or similar learning needs. That way the development costs can be spread. Banks and building societies are among those that have worked with external providers to tailor programmes of technology- and course-based learning as an aid to introducing new systems or work processes.

> Find out whether your organisation has developed any tailored training recently.
>
> What were its objectives?
>
> Who was the provider?
>
> Why was it decided to approach the training in this way?
>
> What role did the in-house trainer(s) play in design, delivery, administration and evaluation?

Working with providers to develop tailored training introduces yet another dimension into the trainer's role. Instead of

▮ either doing all the design, implementation and administration yourselves, as in traditional in-house programmes

▮ or handing over all but some of the evaluation and recording procedure to the supplier, as with a fully external programme, a partnership must be developed. This entails

▌ establishing clear goals and ways of measuring results and progress. The specific learning objectives will be one input, but there may be others – such as prototyping the methodology or creating an in-house capability to deliver future programmes

▌ setting up a 'project plan' to identify the tasks to be completed in the design, testing, administration, delivery and evaluation of the programme – with critical deadlines and milestones

▌ clarifying roles and responsibilities at the outset, setting out exactly who will do what, and when

▌ monitoring progress regularly to ensure deadlines and quality targets are met.

In addition, one or more trainers may be involved in setting up a mutual familiarisation programme – to enable external members of the team to understand your organisation and its goals for the project, and vice versa. Someone will need to make sure the consultants have access to all the people and information they need. Someone will need to review the drafts of content, exercises, tests and other components to make sure their style, language, level, and the messages they contain, are compatible with what you want.

Someone will have to monitor how the bills are mounting, schedule review meetings, handle correspondence. Someone will have to nominate the first cohort of trainees (or guinea pigs) taking account of the specific objectives of each test run. And someone, ultimately, will have to take on the administration and evaluation of the activity once it becomes a regular part of the company training scene.

Roles and responsibilities

As in so many other areas of training, the border between line manager and trainer can readily become blurred when choosing training suppliers. Some managers will have strong views about what is appropriate. Some may take some persuading that a course which has always been run by an external provider could now be delivered equally effectively and at much lower cost in-house. Others may be equally convinced that any external provider would take so long getting to know the business, charge so much and introduce so much irrelevant material to justify it, that it would be better to do it internally.

The role of the trainer in these discussions has to be that of dispassionate professional. Ultimately what matters most is the achievement of the agreed learning objectives. Bringing line managers or colleagues back to these as frequently as is necessary may be your main contribution to the debate.

Clearly it makes no sense to use external resources in preference to internal if that means the latter will be under-used or decay. In the last analysis, whoever holds the training budget will probably make the final decision. If that is to use external suppliers, in whole or in part, that does not mean that everyone inside the organisation can wash their hands of that activity. Instead, as we saw in the last section, each piece of external training, whether for individuals or for groups, should be managed as a mini-project – with the roles of the trainee, his or her boss, the training provider and the in-house trainer/administrator clearly defined. As we have seen, there are plenty of things for 'someone' to do. If you are to be part of the training function, that someone could be you.

Table 10 on page 96 sets out some of the expectations the parties to external training may have of each other.

Table 10

EXPECTATIONS OF PARTIES TO EXTERNAL TRAINING

In-house trainer may be expected to provide:	Line manager may expect to be invited to:	External provider may expect to be given:
collection, collation, cataloguing and evaluation of external training information	participate in objective-setting and evaluation	clear objectives or a brief which includes work to clarify them
up-to-date knowledge of, or access to, information about local courses	contribute ideas and information to help shape the content	realistic timetables for design and delivery
speedy identification of possible external providers	take part in some of the training – to test it or to show support for the trainer and the trainees, to evaluate it or (sometimes) to learn	efficient fulfilment of those parts of the activity being delivered or administered internally
efficient liaison with providers		prompt payment of invoices
efficient administration of all training, external and internal		

In brief

- The basic choice when selecting training providers is between internal and external sources.
- The criteria for choice between the two, and between possible external providers, should be thought through and applied systematically. They will probably include:
  - ☐ reputation/competence ☐ cost
  - ☐ fit with values ☐ location
  - ☐ exclusivity ☐ availability.
- The choice between possible internal providers should be based on
  - ☐ subject expertise ☐ credibility

- coaching skills
- commitment

- availability
- competence in using learning methods.

▌ When using external providers, the relative advantages of open and tailored training should be considered. Open courses have the advantage of exposing trainees to delegates from other organisations, and can cost-effectively provide subject specialists. They can, however, lack focus and make it harder for the trainee to transfer the learning back into the work situation.

▌ Working with external providers, whether on a tailored or open basis, requires absolute clarity about who is going to do what, when and to what standard.

7

Designing a
Training Programme

Introduction

We have not, in previous chapters, tried to distinguish between

▌ one-off learning events to meet specific objectives and

▌ training programmes

Here we will focus on the latter.

> A training programme is a series of linked events designed, when completed, to equip people with the range of competencies needed to do a whole job.

Training programmes may be mounted using exclusively on-job or exclusively off-job learning, or a combination of both. They may also involve internal or external providers, or both. Some are relatively short in duration. It may take an induction programme lasting only a few days to introduce an already competent recruit into a relatively small organisation. Others may last several years. Some senior management development programmes, incorporating study for an MBA, internal and external secondments and projects and specific career moves, would fall into the second category.

In this chapter we shall consider a few of the most common training programmes. You may encounter others – but the trainer's role is likely to remain broadly similar.

Specifically, we shall look at

∎ common features
∎ induction programmes
∎ technical and professional training programmes
∎ apprenticeships and youth training
∎ management and supervisory training schemes
∎ individual programmes.

Common features

Most types of programme have the following in common:

∎ multiple linked objectives – often, but not always, relating to a group rather than one person. 'What are the competencies needed to become an effective branch manager?' is a more likely starting point than 'How can we help branch managers to utilise all the functions of the new point-of-sale equipment?'

∎ a combination of learning methods – and perhaps providers. In some instances the programme will be largely on-job, with courses or other off-job events relatively few and far between. In others, particularly those linked to qualifications, the off-job elements may effectively determine the work to be done between courses

∎ some form of 'programme management' to ensure each element is planned at an appropriate point in the learning sequence and takes place as scheduled

∎ regular reviews of progress to ensure that each element, and the programme as a whole, is delivering the required learning, and to ensure that each trainee is progressing as expected. Trainees who fall behind or fail to make the grade may be removed from the programme

∎ (generally) an expectation that the programme will be undertaken by more than one trainee, either simultaneously or over time. There are exceptions –

where an induction programme is specifically tailored to the needs of one person, or a particular individual is being groomed for a specific role. We shall consider these shortly.

The main steps involved are outlined in Figure 3, and explained in more detail below.

Figure 3

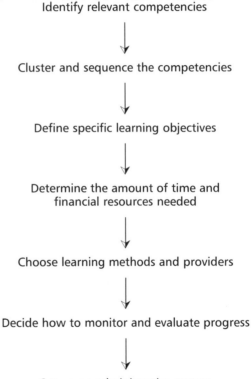

DESIGNING A TRAINING PROGRAMME

Identify relevant competencies

Cluster and sequence the competencies

Define specific learning objectives

Determine the amount of time and financial resources needed

Choose learning methods and providers

Decide how to monitor and evaluate progress

Set up an administrative system

Identify relevant competencies

In Chapter 3 we reviewed some ways of identifying competencies needed in particular roles. This must be the starting point for any programme intended to prepare people for those roles. Whether the goal is to produce a 'cadre' of supervisors, technical experts or general managers, the programme cannot take shape until the designer has a clear and, hopefully, accurate picture of what these roles involve and what it takes to perform in them effectively.

Cluster and sequence the competencies

to identify the possible shape of the overall programme. Trainees will not be able to master everything at once. Some aspects may be linked by common concepts or skills. Mastery of some may depend on having first mastered others. Programmes that have been run in the same form for many years may need review to make sure these internal relationships are still valid.

Define specific learning objectives

for each aspect, to define the level of competence required – see Chapter 4.

Determine the amount of time and financial resources needed

This may have to be 'negotiated' to produce an appropriate cost-benefit pay-back. Some managers are wary of long and elaborate programmes which appear to cost a lot and provide little return beyond an impressive CV for participants. Others take a more philosophical view.

Choose learning methods and providers

– see Chapters 5 and 6 – with the twin aims of providing an effective means of achieving each objective and providing an appropriate mix of approaches.

Decide how to monitor and evaluate progress

– for individuals, each cohort of trainees, and the programme overall. In some cases the formality of examinations may be appropriate – during or at the end of the programme. In others, some form of self-review, perhaps with a learning-log or diary in which trainees note key learning outcomes, may be better.

Set up an administrative system

to ensure that trainees, their managers and other interested parties know what is happening, and when.

The examples that follow illustrate how this applies in practice.

Induction programmes

Whenever a new recruit joins there are likely to be new things to learn. Some of these may be common to all:

▮ company vision and values
▮ company objectives
▮ who's who in the company
▮ what to do in the event of fire or an accident
▮ holiday and sickness arrangements
▮ company rules.

Others will be specific to particular departments

▮ location of fire exits
▮ names of first aiders
▮ departmental objectives
▮ who's who in the department
▮ specific hours of work, meal breaks and rules of conduct.

Yet others will be unique to the job. The size of this last category will depend on how the skills and knowledge required differ from those the recruit already has. Even if the gap is narrow the working processes are unlikely to be identical and the people and locations involved are certainly different. The size of the difference determines the amount of training that will be needed.

Think back to when you began work in your current role.

What sort of induction did you receive?

How effective was it?

How could it have been improved?

In some cases the trainer may have been involved in recruitment. This is particularly likely where there are specific training schemes – for management, technical or other trainees (see below). In that case the induction programme will often be common to all those entering the scheme. For other recruits, the trainer is more likely to work with the personnel department, if there is one, and the recruiting manager to tailor a general programme to individual needs. The sort of tasks you may encounter in developing an induction programme include

Task	Process
researching the needs of people new to the company	may involve interviewing recent recruits to find out how relevant and useful they found their own induction and how they feel about the timing, pace and methods used
reviewing the effectiveness of existing induction	perhaps by talking to line managers, interviewing leavers, or analysing the employee turnover and performance of those who have recently joined
examining other companies' induction programmes	for comparison with your own – perhaps through a formal benchmarking process
undertaking a detailed job analysis	to identify the component tasks of particular jobs, the competencies required and hence the key elements to be addressed during initial training.

In constructing the programme itself it is important to get the right mix of on- and off-job learning. Too much of the latter and the new recruit many feel frustrated that he or she has not 'got started on a proper job'.

It is also important to involve the right people – preferably those the new recruit needs to know – such as the MD or the general manager and his or her own boss – and to use the right mix of methods. Particularly where recruits will go through a standard programme one or two at a time it is tempting to manage some of the delivery through videos or other remote media. Although this has its place, it may not be what the newcomer will most value. In the first few disorienting weeks of a new job, personal contact and the knowledge that 'someone cares' may provide a firmer foundation for the employment relationship than a few hi-tech messages from senior managers. A buddy system, where an experienced employee partners the new recruit, shows them around, introduces them to others and answers their questions can be useful here.

Your role in operating the induction programme could range from planning and co-ordinating it to actual delivery. In some organisations the apparently routine nature of induction means that even those relatively inexperienced in training may be asked to manage the programme or conduct elements of it. Others recognise the vital importance of first impressions and involve only their most experienced trainers. It is pointless to spend hundreds – even thousands – of pounds on recruitment only to turn people off through inept induction.

Technical and professional training programmes

Some organisations offer a limited number of training places each year to help ensure that there will always be enough people coming through the business who are competent in core activities. Engineering firms, for example, may offer technical traineeships, and firms of accountants or lawyers offer professional traineeships.

Table 11

POSSIBLE TRAINER INVOLVEMENT IN TECHNICAL AND PROFESSIONAL PROGRAMMES

Area of involvement	Explanation
Design	Work with specialists inside and outside the organisation to design a programme with the right mix of current practice, future developments and leading-edge thinking.
Investigate funding	Find out what funding or financial support may be available for all or part of the programme, especially if it is geared to attaining an NVQ. Local 'Business Links' are the first port of call for this.
Negotiate	Negotiate with external providers and funding bodies, such as the Training and Enterprise Council (TEC).
Administer	Administer funding or attendance arrangements.
Recruit	Assist either in an administrative capacity, placing advertisements, organising interviews and assessment days and the associated correspondence with candidates – or as a selector yourself.
Monitor	Monitor the programme, including trainee attendance and standards achieved.
Act as counsellor to the trainees	Be someone they can turn to for advice if they are finding things difficult or whose help they can seek in, for example, getting more support from their line manager in the on-job elements.
Act as 'placement officer'	Find suitable projects or secondments for trainees. These may be internal or external, and will involve making sure both sides understand the terms of reference and each other's expectations. You may also fulfil a similar role at the end of the programme if it is necessary to act as 'broker' for first appointments with line managers who may not know any of the trainees well.
Evaluate the programme	Do this in the medium and long term. This could mean detailed analytical work tracking the career and salary progression of former trainees to identify retention and promotion rates and see whether the programme overall is achieving its goals.

Sometimes entry to such schemes is drawn direct from colleges or universities. Sometimes it is open to more experienced candidates from inside or outside the business. Sometimes schemes are designed and operated on the basis of the requirements of a single company. Sometimes consortia will join together and involve colleges, universities or other external providers in delivery. Occasionally sandwich courses at university form an integral part of the programme. Sometimes programmes lead to an externally recognised qualification. Sometimes a company certificate or diploma is awarded. Sometimes 'graduation' to a particular role or level in the organisation marks the end of the programme.

> How does your organisation ensure it has an appropriate supply of technically competent individuals to carry the business forward?
>
> Is there a technical training scheme?
>
> If so, how effective is it?
>
> If not, should there be one?

Unless you are a technical expert in your own right you are not likely to be directly involved in conducting such programmes, but you are likely to have a role in their management or administration. In particular, you may need to do some or all of the things listed in Table 11.

Apprenticeships and Youth Training

'Time-served' apprentice schemes used to be the only means of entry to a career as a craftsman. The on-job training received during the four- or five-year term was sometimes variable in quality but some consistency of standards was provided by the City and Guilds or other examinations for the day, evening or block-release classes that underpinned them.

Today's Modern Apprentices are more likely to be on shorter programmes agreed between the trainee, the TEC and the employer. Even so the combination of on- and off-job learning is still a key feature, as is the attainment of a recognised qualification – at NVQ Level 3 or above.

Although Modern Apprenticeships are gradually gaining ground, Youth Training for 16- and 17-year-olds is well-established. Here, too, there is a programme of on- and off-job learning to be designed, administered and delivered to ensure trainees develop the necessary personal and job skills to equip them for their working lives. Your organisation may be involved in managing a scheme directly, or work in partnership with others to provide the work experience elements of the programme.

For both programmes there is a considerable amount of administrative support required. Careful records of plans, payments and progress must be kept, especially where TEC funding is involved. The progress of individual trainees must be carefully monitored and close contact maintained with all the other parties. You may be involved in any or all of the ways outlined in Table 11 – with the added complexity that the use of taxpayers' money inevitably brings.

Management and supervisory training schemes

These, like technical and professional schemes can be run wholly internally or partly externally. They may or may not entail work towards formal qualifications. Some organisations have several such schemes, ranging from a senior manager or even director level development programme down to direct entry schemes for those with A levels or degrees. We shall focus on the more junior end of this spectrum.

> Does your organisation operate a graduate training scheme?
>
> If so, how is the training programme structured?
>
> If not, what would be the possible advantages and disadvantages of introducing one?

The length and content of such programmes varies, as do the expectations of the participants regarding their medium- and long-term career destinations. In many organisations, graduate schemes in particular have had a somewhat chequered history:

- When times are hard recruitment may be cut back or even stopped altogether.

- Those who joined the organisation to do a job rather than to get on a 'fast-track' scheme sometimes resent their high profile colleagues – leading some employers to offer such access to existing employees as well as those fresh from the education system.

- The difficulty of predicting potential in candidates in their late teens and early twenties has meant that some schemes have a high drop-out rate. Sometimes this is because trainees decide they have made the wrong career choice. Sometimes it is because the employer decides they have selected someone who will not make the grade.

- The nature of management and supervisory roles is changing rapidly in some organisations. Some of those who have come through the scheme may not, after all, be competent to fill key roles in the business tomorrow. This may throw into question the design and content of the whole programme.

As a trainer concerned to ensure the future, as well as the present, skill base of your organisation you will need constantly to question the objectives of such schemes and their link with other programmes of employee development. With your line management colleagues, and possibly with external help, you should check periodically to make sure the competencies the programme was designed to develop are still relevant to the emerging needs of the organisation. This may affect:

Recruitment to the scheme

Are some degree disciplines more relevant than others? Do some educational establishments produce candidates better suited to your needs? Someone may need to do some detailed analysis of past intakes to find out.

The expectations you seek to create

Are all your communications with potential recruits realistic and consistent – from the first advertisement in a careers directory, through any leaflets or brochures you lodge with careers offices, to the language used by everyone they meet at interview and during other phases of selection – right through the induction process?

The design of the programme

Are the specific learning objectives of each element clear, explicit and relevant? Is it clear how achievement will be measured at each stage? Are the links between on- and off-job components clear and understood by those concerned with each? Research to identify any mismatches could be part of your role. So, too, could be study of participant reactions to particular parts of the programme.

Learning methods

Are these in line with participant expectations? For those who have been used to 24-hour access to PCs for private study using computer-based training modules, a return to a tutor-centred 'chalk and talk' approach could seem quaint or patronising. If it is not what they expected at the start of a high-flying career they may start looking for a more progressive employer. Even if trainees appear happy to settle back and be 'spoon-fed', you will need to find ways of increasing their self-reliance and responsibility for their own learning. Coaching can be a key element of this.

Tutors' styles and approaches

Are you using your brightest and best people to provide role models and inspire commitment? Or are you fielding the second, or even the third, XI – people who have failed in line management roles or have time on their hands for other reasons – such as impending retirement. Are they providing enough intellectual stimulation – or merely an entertaining diversion?

As well as demanding high standards of design and delivery, management and supervisory trainees are likely to need just the same level of emotional and administrative support as technical trainees. This may extend to help in finding accommodation if they are new to the area. The administration of relocation arrangements could therefore be part of your brief.

As with technical trainees, relationships will need to be established with local providers to arrange day or block release for qualification courses such as the Diploma in Management Studies (DMS) or National Examining Board for Supervisory Management (NEBSM) Certificate. If the programme is large enough, a special variant may be tailored for your organisation. This will allow potentially greater flexibility of pace and content. It will, however, deprive your trainees of the chance to mix with those from other organisations – which can be particularly beneficial at this stage in their careers.

Individual programmes

These take two main forms:

Tailored versions of general programmes

Some organisations modify their technical, professional,

management or supervisory training programmes to suit the needs of particular individuals. Thus a graduate with a business studies degree may skip those parts of the management training programme which would duplicate learning already acquired. In that case, someone may have to check the detailed syllabus content and performance criteria to make sure the trainee will not miss out. Someone will also have to weigh up whether it is better for the whole group to follow the training programme together or allow an element of 'pick and mix'.

Unique programmes

If your company recruits a new chief executive with no experience of your particular industry, neither your planned open training events nor your management or technical training scheme may quite fit the bill. The depth and breadth of knowledge required, and the speed with which learning will have to take place are likely to be rather different from those of your average trainee. That is not to say that modules from existing training cannot be included or adapted if they fit his or her needs. What it does mean is that the essential elements of what the business is about and how it works at present must be conveyed quickly and effectively. This may require a programme of visits, one-to-one meetings and access to financial reports and business planning documents – rather than any sort of 'course'.

> Talk to someone who has recently been recruited into your organisation at a relatively senior level.
>
> Find out what sort of individual training, if any, they have had since joining.
>
> Are they aware of any formal programme to help them?
>
> What would be the pros and cons of creating such a programme?

The need for this sort of programme does not arise very often. Much more common is the situation where an individual is identified as having some, but not all, of the competencies needed for a particular role and wishes to develop the rest. Development centres, which we discussed in Chapter 3, are designed to highlight such instances.

Because each person's profile of competencies will be different, each will need an individually tailored programme. This may comprise new on-job experiences, perhaps via internal secondment, or coaching to gain more from the existing job. It may also include attendance at specific external programmes – perhaps at a national or international business school. One or more of the open events in the company training calendar may also be appropriate – or a special course for those with a shared need could be devised.

Whatever the content of the programme, the process for developing it will generally follow the pattern outlined at the beginning of this chapter. In particular, clarity of objectives and initial expectations is crucial. If the individual believes that success in the training programme will lead to promotion while the company believes it may stave off dismissal, there could be problems ahead.

The individual nature of these programmes may pose particular challenges for the trainer – especially when it comes to planning, time-tabling and evaluating. It is generally much easier to keep track of 20 people doing 10 things together than of 10 people doing 20 things separately. As so often in training, the efficiency of the administration process could count for as much as the effectiveness of specific learning events.

Roles and responsibilities

The role played by line managers in designing and delivering the sort of training discussed here varies widely. Without their regular and well thought through input, none of these programmes is likely to achieve relevant goals. The role of the trainer is likely to involve

■ reviewing the goals and present reality of such programmes in the ways outlined above

■ researching best practice in other organisations to make sure that the programmes offered stand comparison with competitors in terms of content, quality and rewards

■ identifying and recommending improvements

■ designing and implementing simple, effective, non-bureaucratic internal administration procedures – to keep line management paper-work to a minimum while ensuring total transparency of who is, has been, or will be at which stage of the programme, when and with what results.

Line managers will generally expect the trainer to

■ establish contact with appropriate external providers and funding bodies

■ be proactive in identifying added-value, low cost options – such as a link with an appropriate awarding body for a diploma, certificate or NVQ

■ establish trainees' eligibility for such elements of the programme

■ (perhaps) assist in recruitment to training schemes. If there is a personnel manager who handles such matters for the rest of the business he or she will want to make sure that the terms offered and the procedures followed are consistent with those elsewhere in the organisation. Responsibility for ensuring that the equal opportunities policy is adhered to may rest with the personnel department and they will not be prepared to countenance any recruitment strategies which might compromise particular groups.

In brief

▌ A training programme comprises a series of linked events designed to equip people with the range of competencies needed to do a whole job.

▌ They may be exclusively on-job, exclusively off-job, or a mixture and may include a range of different learning methods.

▌ Programmes require management and regular review.

▌ Most will be undertaken by more than one trainee, either simultaneously or over time. Individually tailored programmes arising from development centres are one exception to this.

▌ Designing a programme involves identifying relevant competencies, clustering and sequencing them, defining specific learning objectives, determining resources, choosing learning methods and providers, deciding how to monitor and evaluate and setting up an administrative system.

▌ The most common types are
  ▢ induction
  ▢ technical and professional training schemes
  ▢ Modern Apprenticeships and Youth Training
  ▢ management and supervisory training schemes.

▌ Developing an induction programme may entail, researching needs, reviewing effectiveness, benchmarking with other companies or undertaking detailed job analysis.

▌ The trainer's involvement with technical, professional, management and supervisory programmes may include:
  ▢ design
  ▢ investigating funding
  ▢ negotiating funding
  ▢ administration

☐   recruitment
☐   monitoring
☐   acting as counsellor to the trainees
☐   acting as 'placement officer'
☐   evaluating the programme.

8

Conducting a Training Session

Introduction

Chapter 5 highlighted the distinction between tutor-centred and learner-centred training and some of the issues involved in choosing learning methods. In summary, the choice of method should be dictated by the learning objectives to be achieved and the learning styles of the participants. In most cases a combination of approaches is likely to be called for.

In this chapter we shall look at what is involved in using

∎ presentations
∎ visual aids
∎ coaching
∎ practical exercises
∎ role plays
∎ case-studies.

– pointing out some of the demands they make on the would-be trainer. You will find further discussion in *Delivering Training* by Suzy Siddons. Where practical exercises, role plays and case-studies are used, the quality of the debriefing process is crucial. We shall devote a separate section to this.

Preparation

Whichever method is to be used, careful preparation is essential. The elements to consider are:

- content
- method
- location
- timing.

Content

What trainees must learn will, of course, depend on the specific objectives to be achieved. The possible range is huge. Selection interviewing, presentation skills, the application of the organisation's equal opportunities policy, handling disciplinary problems, getting the best out of others, assertiveness, working in teams, project management, understanding the balance sheet, financial appraisal, selling skills, product features, advantages and benefits, telephone skills, letter writing, report writing, negotiating skills – arc just some of the non-technical subjects typically covered on in-house courses.

Add to these the use of specific work processes and information: from how to read an international timetable – in the travel industry; to how to check for forged bank notes and what to do if you find one – in sales; to how to set up, maintain or operate particular equipment – from electronic point of sale tills to satellite dishes and from water meters to catalytic converters, the list could go on for pages.

A few of these subjects are likely to be relevant regardless of the nature of the business. Many will be specific to the industry or company. If you are to be involved in running training sessions, the depth and breadth of your competence and confidence in dealing with the subject matter is important. There are few things more unnerving for an inexperienced trainer than being caught out on questions of fact – and few things transmit themselves more easily than uncertainty. You will need to be able to

■ *consider the subject from a number of different angles* (past, present and future, comparison with other organisations, background theory, legislation, in-company examples and statistics may all be relevant)
■ *break it down to its essentials* (to expose the underlying principles)
■ *separate the important from the trivial* (the 'must know' from the 'should know' and the 'could know').

You do not need to be a world expert on every subject. In fact knowing too much can sometimes be as bad as knowing too little, if it stops you from starting where the trainees are. Knowing your audience can be just as important as knowing your subject. You will have to learn to pitch your material at the right level. Aim too high and you will lose everyone in the first five minutes; too low and your audience will not only learn nothing, they may feel they are being patronised. A few check questions at the beginning, to make sure you've got it about right, are always useful. You need to know how to react if it turns out you got it wrong – the next section will help.

As you get more experienced and skilled in helping others learn, you will find you can do this even in areas you know comparatively little about or where your audience is more knowledgeable than you. The questions you ask, and the awareness you raise, may be enough. But to begin with you will want to feel you have a solid grasp, particularly if you are using any form of tutor-centred learning.

Method

Effective preparation should cover the 'how' as well as the 'what'. Whichever method is to be used, the trainer should be competent in handling it. Unless you have been trained to use a particular method, it is better to leave it alone. Even when you are experienced, it will require careful forethought to ensure that you introduce and debrief in a way that adds to learning. We shall consider the specifics as we examine each method.

Location

Sorting out where to conduct your session and getting it set up appropriately will also require thought. Most of the methods considered in this chapter imply off-job learning. For most you will need a training room that is

■ light and airy

■ quiet and free from distractions (including telephones)

■ equipped with flexible, easily moved furniture to allow a range of possible layouts, from a simple semicircle of chairs, through 'cabaret style' where sets of four to six people can sit round tables, to more formal 'horseshoes' of tables and chairs

■ furnished with screen, whiteboard, flip chart(s), overhead projector and (for role play and some practical exercises) video cameras and playback facilities, plus the necessary power sources and blackout arrangements

■ provided with 'Blu-Tack'-friendly walls or plenty of board space to pin up flip chart paper

■ big enough to accommodate the whole learning group, and supported by separate syndicate rooms if necessary.

Timing

Your session will be most effective if it is conducted when trainees are ready for it – that is when

■ any necessary prior learning has taken place

■ they are in a position to go back and use what they have learnt

■ they are likely to be at their most receptive. The session immediately after lunch is popularly held to be the 'graveyard shift'. It is not a good idea to make a formal presentation then if you can avoid it, in case your audience decide to sleep off their lunch instead of listening to you. Reserve that slot for more active exercises and tasks which will force trainees to move around.

Views differ about the value of evening work on residential courses. Some regard the more relaxed social interaction which takes place after dinner as a means of building a sense of belonging to the organisation and a useful chance to broaden understanding of each other's roles and of the business. Others see it as idle time at the company's expense and insist on project work or syndicate sessions. Your task will be to ensure that the effectiveness of learning is not jeopardised by bad scheduling.

You will also need to ensure that there is sufficient time for each element of the session. When learners are engrossed in practical work or role plays, some careful time-management may be required to make sure that the debriefing is not rushed to the detriment of real learning.

Making a presentation

In spite of the wide range of other methods now being used, 'input sessions' of one sort or another still have a role to play. The formal or informal presentation of information and ideas can be used as a stand-alone vehicle to enhance knowledge. Alternatively, with the use of questions on both sides, it can provide a basis for a more broadly based exploration of the subject.

The effectiveness of a presentation depends on the clarity of its objectives and the extent to which the audience buy into them. If the presenter's aim is to win an 'Oscar' and the audience are there to find out about the subject, the two may or may not be compatible.

▌ Tell them what you're going to tell them.

▌ Tell them.

▌ Tell them you've told them.

Structuring a presentation around these principles may

be a rather traditional approach – but it works. It means you will need to be able to:

■ summarise the structure and key points at the start – see below

■ present the content in a way that captures the attention and imagination of your audience

■ reinforce this at the end to make sure that trainees go away with the right message.

Unless your presentation is to be very short – and most people's attention span is less than 20 minutes – you may need to use other media to help. We shall consider the role of visual aids in the next section. If you see yourself as a possible presenter you will need as many as possible of the characteristics outlined in Table 12 on page 122.

Most of these can be learnt through practice and feedback. Your starting point needs to be a well constructed presentation skills course, where you can learn to reconcile the demands of effective presentation with your own personal style. You will find some suggestions at the end of this chapter. In addition you will need to

■ structure your material to build in a framework to help people remember. Especially if you have a bit of a butterfly mind, hopping from one idea to another, you may find it hard to get other people to follow your line of thought. Some subjects lend themselves to a chronological approach, others can be looked at from the perspective of different people, yet others may follow a 'who, what, why, how, when, where' sequence. Sometimes it will be necessary to work through the material several times, putting key points on 'Post-its' which can be clustered and re-clustered until an appropriate framework emerges.

■ build in signposts to help the audience follow your structure and remember it. You can do this by outlining it at the beginning and then regularly drawing attention to where you have got to. Visual aids can help here – see below.

Table 12

CHARACTERISTICS OF EFFECTIVE PRESENTERS

Characteristic	Explanation
A clear and pleasant speaking voice	This should convey enthusiasm for the subject without sounding 'over the top' and sincerity without sounding superficial, and rise and fall naturally to retain interest.
No distracting verbal mannerisms	Repeated use of any phrase can distract your audience – the least interested will be counting the repetitions rather than listening to the content. Particularly irritating are 'you know', 'sort of', 'actually', and 'you know what I mean'.
No distracting physical mannerisms	Fiddling nervously with a paper clip, jewellery or a pen, playing with your hair, scratching, or waving your arms can be distracting if taken to extremes. Controlling these, perhaps by putting one hand firmly in your pocket at the start of the session, is something you will learn on a presentation skills course.
Personal 'presence'	This is required to draw the attention of your audience and make them want to listen. If you are too timid or uncertain they will not take you seriously. If you are too dogmatic or pushy they may react negatively.
Empathy with and interest in your audience	If you do not care whether they listen and learn, they may not either. If you cannot help them feel involved in the subject, they may find it easier not to be involved.
Effective questioning skills	It is very useful to ask questions of your audience as an aid to establishing empathy and rapport, checking how best to make your material really relevant, and testing reactions and understanding. (New trainers sometimes find it hard to phrase their questions in the right way. They do not want to make it too obvious what answer they are looking for, lest the audience feel they are playing guessing games. On the other hand, if the question is worded too indirectly or clumsily they will not see what you're driving at.)

▌ rehearse. You need to know how long your presentation takes. You need to experience how it sounds when spoken out loud. Ideally you need to get feedback from a 'guinea-pig' to help you identify points that need clarification and to give you feedback about the pace and volume of your delivery.

Making a good presentation takes time and patience as well as skill and, above all, meticulous planning. It also requires the ability to think on your feet. If your questions highlight that your audience are on a different wavelength, you will have to decide whether to plod on anyway or try to tailor your presentation accordingly. If their questions to you seem to be going back over old ground, you will have to decide whether to repeat the key points, try to restate them in a different way, ask another member of the group if he or she can summarise the issue, or tell the questioner off for not listening.

> Choose a topic that interests you – perhaps a hobby or a particular project at work.
>
> Decide who you would like as an audience and the objectives you would like to set.
>
> Prepare a 10-minute presentation and rehearse it.
>
> If you can, find a tame audience of one or more people to whom you can make your presentation.

If your audience challenges the view you have been putting forward, you will have to decide whether to leap to your own defence, enter into a debate, or try to understand the questioner's perspective. When you've spent hours preparing what you thought was the definitive last word on the subject, it can be disconcerting when someone appears to disagree. You must be able to depersonalise the issue and see all questions as expressions of interest rather than challenges or threats.

Using visual aids

Visual aids take several forms, including

- prepared or spontaneous viewfoils or acetates for the overhead projector (OHP)
- prepared or spontaneous flip chart pages

▮ posters
▮ video clips
▮ interactive multi-media.

Our focus here is mainly on the first two.

Sometimes the presenter will be expected to prepare and use aids him- or herself. Sometimes a specialist does it. Either way it involves

▮ thinking carefully about the objectives and content of the presentation

▮ deciding which are the key messages

▮ identifying ways of adding to, rather than detracting from the presentation – in a memorable and compelling way

▮ designing and producing materials in the required format. This may mean drawing freehand, using a word processing or desk top publishing package or one of the numerous specialist computer graphics packages now available. You may be able to prepare all the material before the presentation – or only the basic layout. Audience comments, data supplied on the day, and other last minute inputs may be addressed on the spot.

It is beyond dispute that most presentations benefit from good visual aids. Most people have far better recall of information that they have seen *and* heard than of hearing alone. Even so, it is easy to overdo it or confuse.

If you are involved in this sort of work, either to support your own presentations or other people's, you will find Jacqui Gough's detailed guidance in *Developing Learning Materials* very helpful. Far too many presenters seem to think that a page of the company accounts, photocopied on to acetate and flashed on a screen for 30 seconds is illuminating. In fact, tightly packed figures are the worst form of visual aid – followed closely by tightly packed sentences.

The best visual aids take the message and present it

graphically – in a bar or pie-chart for example, with a clear legend and key, or pictorially, with photographs of products or illustrations of concepts.

If you are delivering a presentation using visual aids the pitfalls are many and various. They range from the apparently trivial – such as spelling mistakes and bad handwriting – to obscuring the audience's view – to giving one message orally while the audience are struggling to read something different on the screen or flip chart.

> Decide what visual aids would make your 10-minute presentation more memorable and compelling.
>
> Prepare them.

Again, training and practice will be the keys to effective usage – provided you never lose sight of the fact that the latest technicolour, virtual-reality, transient-image gismo is only of value if it really does aid learning. If the audience will be lost in wonder at the technology rather than receiving the message it is designed to convey, as a trainer you will have failed.

Coaching

In Chapter 5 we identified the main elements of coaching and highlighted some of its uses. It is obviously dangerous to put forward one method as a panacea for all learning needs. The basic principles of coaching are such, though, that it comes close to being just that. Even if you are presenting to, or using practical exercises with, groups you can focus their attention and raise their awareness through questions designed to allow the learner to explore a situation or experience a task.

To be an effective coach you will need to foster the following skills:

■ a willingness to start from where the learner is and

follow his or her interests

■ questioning skills

■ listening skills

■ summarising skills

■ clarity of thought

■ good powers of concentration

■ determination to draw ideas and solutions from the learner

■ a sense of humour

■ persistence and follow-through – to make sure the trainees really do commit to action

■ integrity – not to divulge what you learn from trainees

■ patience – to restart the process as often as necessary

■ will power – not to impose your own ideas and solutions.

As we shall see in Chapter 10, many of these abilities are essential not only for coaching but also for the increasingly important role that the trainer may play as an internal consultant.

Practical exercises

Practical exercises put real trainees in real or simulated situations. They take many forms. From practice sessions on workplace machinery to interactive media-based activity; from business simulations to outdoor leadership and team-building tasks. The range, again, is huge. At a general level the objectives may be similar. That is, to provide an opportunity for the trainees to learn through experience rather than on the basis of abstract theory alone.

Herein lies the key to the effective use of such exercises. Experience alone may teach us very little. It is reflection on that experience and the chance to work out alternative ways of tackling it before trying again that really moves people around the learning cycle. Whether it is designed to help a trainee accountant construct a budget or a trainee manager lead a team in a crisis, the exercise itself will be only part of the learning experience.

With this in mind, practical exercises should be approached as a means to an end rather than as ends in themselves. Beware the trainer who sets the group up with an exercise and then goes off to do something else while they get on with it. It may not be necessary for the trainer to breathe down trainees' necks all the time, but he or she almost certainly needs to be available

- to clarify the brief and the objectives
- to advise on resources to help
- to observe any points of confusion not deliberately built into the exercise
- especially in the case of outdoor and machine-based exercises, to ensure the safety of trainees
- to coach and debrief after the event to help trainees reflect and draw out key learning.

Do not be misled into thinking that setting exercises is the easy way of training. Physically, mentally and emotionally it can be much more demanding than a few hours lecturing or presenting. If, for example, you get involved in outdoor training exercises, you may have to do any or all of the following:

- Scour the countryside for suitable routes for teams to follow.
- Go out at dawn to plant clues.
- Lie buried in mouldy leaves while the teams search for a 'body'.
- Hire, issue and account for special equipment – from mobile phones to tents and sleeping bags.
- Man a check-point – usually somewhere wet and windy.
- Act as liaison point for information.

All this may be in addition to managing early morning

briefing sessions and late night debriefing. These can themselves be far more difficult to manage effectively than they may look. Trainees are often wound up and it may be hard to control the flow and direct the discussion to the really relevant areas of learning – and harder still to help people relate that to some general framework of behaviour that they can use back at work. It does not matter how cold or hungry the trainees felt. The question is what effect did that have on the way they behaved towards each other, and what are the parallels at work? Drawing that out will require considerable coaching skills when the members of the group just want to tell you how miserable they are.

Planning and executing such exercises is obviously not a job for a lone novice. It is, nevertheless, part of what may be required of you as your career develops. To some, this is the exciting end of training. To others, it sounds like living hell. Either way, there is a real danger in focusing on the exercises themselves rather than the learning they are designed to achieve. If you do get involved in designing exercises of any sort you will need to

∎ be fully conversant with the learning objectives
∎ understand the competencies to be developed
∎ have the imagination to create situations or scenarios where such competencies can be tested or developed
∎ have the attention to detail to make sure there are no accidental inconsistencies in the information given to participants.

Role plays

Role plays require one or more of the trainees to assume a role other than their own. Many sales training courses, for instance, include role playing of customers. Some safety awareness courses put trainees in the role of supervisor or safety trainer. Some interview skills courses put trainees in the role of candidate, aggrieved employee or appraisee.

What all have in common is their objectives. By asking someone to play a role other than their own, it is possible to help them see the world from a different perspective. The safety trainer required to persuade a colleague to wear personal protective equipment may, in the process of marshalling the arguments, convince him- or herself. The 'customer' who has been shabbily treated by the company may begin to understand some of the tensions and anxieties customers feel when they come to complain.

At the same time, the other participants in the role play should develop their competence in dealing with such situations. The sales person learns how to deal with an irate customer. The manager learns to conduct an effective interview. Many trainees find role plays provide invaluable interpersonal and attitude skills training.

Some, though, find role playing quite stressful. Others may dismiss it as 'play-acting' with no relevance to real life. Managing a successful session requires careful selection of both material and participants, ample briefing and skilled debriefing to help participants confront their learning without damaging their self-esteem.

Wherever possible, real life examples should be used. It helps, too, if the person whose skills you are trying to develop is able, so far as possible, to be themselves – acting as they think appropriate to the situation – rather than taking on the personality of some fictitious character.

Writing role plays is yet another skill the trainer may find useful. It calls for

∎ clear understanding of learning objectives/ competencies to be developed
∎ imagination
∎ realism
∎ thoroughness in the preparation of briefing and debriefing materials

▮ attention to detail

▮ reasonable writing skills. You will not need the literary skills of Shakespeare or Dickens. You will need to be able to convey, as briefly and unequivocally as possible, the gist of a situation or problem.

As with any other form of practical exercise, it is not the five minutes or the thirty-five minutes of the role play which are crucial. It is the preparation and follow-up that matter most. The trainer should

▮ plan the time allocation carefully. All participants and observers must have time to give and receive feedback

▮ manage the feedback constructively. It is usually best to ask the key player, the person whose skills you have been trying to develop, to talk through how it felt and what did and did not go according to plan before inviting the other participants to contribute. The observers should then be invited to reflect back what they saw happening, focusing on observed behaviour rather than value judgements, praise or blame. If trainees are not yet 100 per cent competent the quest must be for alternative positive behaviour – what could he or she have done instead? Self-coaching, peer coaching or coaching by the trainer are appropriate.

Structured report forms for all participants and observers can be useful. These will help to create the right tone if they focus on what was actually said or done and its observed effects, rather than on personalities or emotions.

Running a complex role play, involving several participants, each with a different brief, demands attention to administrative detail as well as training skills. As with other practical exercises, you may find that learning that looks quite fun from the trainees' perspective is in fact pretty hard work!

> Get together with a colleague and identify something you have observed him or her doing – conducting an interview or giving a presentation would be ideal, but a smaller task would do.
>
> With your colleague, prepare a checklist of the behaviours you agree are 'good practice' in handling such a situation.
>
> Then give him or her feedback on how he or she actually handled it.
>
> Conclude by asking how helpful your feedback was and how it could have been improved.
>
> (As a variation on this task, and to develop your debriefing skills, try following the six debriefing steps outlined on page 132, before giving your own feedback.)

Case-studies

These may be real or fictitious, written or in video or computerised format. Case-studies typically describe a company or a sequence of events, usually accompanied by relevant numerical and financial information.

Questions on the case may revolve around how the situation arose or could have been avoided and what should be done about it now. Where learning objectives have an analytical element, or where knowledge and understanding can be achieved through study of a particular example, case-studies can be useful. They can be tackled either individually or in groups and reported on in written answers or class presentation. One variation is the incident method. Based on a full case study, this starts by giving trainees only one or two facts. By careful questioning of the tutor or other role players, they have to build up the whole case. This helps to develop questioning and deductive skills.

Although practical exercises and role plays bring out the trainer's creative talents, writing case-studies calls for a more factual, research-oriented approach. Many academic institutions combine their own research in companies with the production of case-studies for their students to learn from. Some company training departments take the same approach, using work in one department or division as a means of spreading best practice to others.

Using case-studies as an aid to learning again calls for good coaching and questioning skills if the trainees' natural tendency to describe rather than analyse is to be avoided.

Debriefing

The key to effective learning, from role plays, practical exercises and case-studies, lies in debriefing. And the key to effective debriefing lies mainly in the objectives. What did you intend that trainees should be able to do after the session? What has happened during the session that has brought them closer to this goal?

As so often, it is the coaching model that is the most appropriate. Clearly the precise form a debrief takes will depend on the nature and content of the exercise. But you will not go far wrong if you remember to do the following:

1 Ask the participants what they saw as their goal(s) in the activity overall and at particular points.
2 Ask them what happened and how that related to the goal(s).
3 Ask them what options they considered to help them achieve their goal(s).
4 Ask them how they decided on a particular option and what criteria they applied.
5 Ask them how the choice of that option has brought them closer to their goal(s).
6 Ask them, on reflection, what, if anything, they think they might have done differently and what effect that might have had on their achievement of the goal(s).

Once those actually engaged in the exercise have been debriefed, observers can be invited to join in. Whether or not you ask them to contribute at each of the six steps outlined above is a matter of judgement. The benefits of allowing them to feel more actively involved must be weighed against any possible distraction from participants' journey around the learning cycle.

Learners who are unused to the type of experiential learning to be derived from these methods may tend to look to you, as tutor, to pass judgement on their performance or to tell them what they should have done differently. It is important that you resist this temptation. Turn the question back on the trainees, if necessary reminding them of key elements of the objectives and taking them back through the six steps. Although formal assessment of performance will sometimes be necessary, try to keep this separate from the learning debrief.

Roles and responsibilities

Many different members of the organisation may need to give presentations. From the MD's induction speech to last year's star trainee giving a 'pep' talk to this year's group, all may look to the trainer to help them by

- making sure the objectives are clear
- advising on length and level of content
- drafting appropriate text
- preparing visual aids
- making sure the location is set up and everything in working order
- making sure the audience is there, on time and with appropriate expectations
- operating specific equipment
- preparing handouts or other supporting material
- distributing handouts
- providing feedback afterwards.

If the presentation is part of a course or programme for which the trainer is responsible, it may also fall to him or her to introduce the speakers, thank them afterwards and follow-up for next time.

How much of the physical preparation falls directly to the trainer depends on resources. Some trainers have to do everything from moving the furniture and putting new pads on the flip chart to writing the content, producing the acetates and photocopying the handouts. In other organisations, as we saw in Chapter 5, the work is shared with administrative and technical support.

Who in your organisation has to make presentations most frequently?

How effectively do they do it?

How could you help?

When it comes to using practical exercises, role plays and case-studies the trainer will usually be expected to take the lead in locating or designing appropriate material – perhaps with input from line managers. Delivery, particularly of large-scale practical exercises, is often team-based, calling for support from line managers, trainers and other specialists, inside and outside the organisation. There is real value in this. The more involved all parties get in helping others learn and in building up a common understanding of what a particular competence looks like in practice, the more likely the behaviour learnt during the course will be transferred back to and reinforced in the workplace.

Coaching, as already discussed, can be done either by line managers or trainers, formally or informally. The more widespread the coaching ethic becomes and the more fully developed the skills, the more likely it is that colleagues will coach each other and their bosses, as well as being coached themselves. When that happens, the organisation is probably well on the way to having what is sometimes referred to as a learning culture – see Chapter 10. It certainly means that any other participative methods – from practical exercises to case-studies, can be debriefed more effectively than might otherwise be the case.

In brief

■ Preparation is crucial.

■ Content, method, location and timing should all be considered in the light of the specific objectives and the audience.

■ Effective presentations need careful structuring and signposting and a sincere interest in the audience – as well as a clear and pleasant voice, an absence of distracting mannerisms and good questioning skills.

  ☐ Tell them what you're going to tell them.

  ☐ Tell them.

  ☐ Then tell them what you've told them.

■ Visual aids, such as viewfoils, flip charts, posters, video clips and multi-media, should reinforce the key messages of the presentation – rather than distract from them.

■ Coaching can be as relevant in group learning as in one-to-one situations.

■ Practical exercises take many forms – from physical outdoor activities to computer simulations and board games.

■ If practical exercises are to be used effectively, clear objectives and careful debriefing are essential.

■ Role plays enable trainees to experience the world through other people's eyes and to practise their interpersonal skills.

■ Writing role plays needs imagination and realism and careful attention to detail. In running them, the objectives and feedback are again key.

∎ Case-studies are best based on fact, and can be a way of spreading good practice.

∎ Debriefing is best done systematically, using the coaching model to explore participants' own reactions before involving observers.

9 Evaluating Training

Introduction

Like any of the other business processes we shall discuss in Chapter 10, the learning process is capable of both continuous improvement and more radical step changes. Unless the process is producing outputs that the business and its customers want and value, it is a waste of time.

> Evaluation is about trying to assess whether or not training is indeed producing relevant and valued outputs through efficient and well-managed processes. It is itself a process – of gathering information with which to make decisions about training activities.

Constant reappraisal of the relevance of the outputs, the quality of the inputs, and the efficiency and effectiveness of the process itself is as important in training as in any other area of business.

In this chapter we shall look at

∎ the purposes of evaluation
∎ evaluation and continuous improvement
∎ different approaches to evaluation
∎ the skills needed
∎ evaluation and Investors in People
∎ roles and responsibilities.

Purposes of evaluation

Evaluation has three main purposes:

Feedback to help trainers understand the extent to which objectives are being met and the effectiveness of particular learning activities – as an aid to continuous improvement (see below)

Control to make sure training policy and practice are aligned with organisational goals and delivering cost-effective solutions to organisational issues

Intervention to raise awareness of key issues such as pre-course and post-course briefing and the selection of delegates

In some organisations it is taken for granted that all training is worthwhile and relatively little effort is devoted to in-depth analysis of its impact. In others, and especially those aspiring to recognition as an Investor in People, establishing the links between training and performance at the business, group and individual level is seen as essential.

Evaluation and continuous improvement

For the trainer, evaluation is itself a learning process. Training which has been planned and delivered is reflected on. Views of how to do it better are formulated and tested – and built in next time around. The outcome may be to

- abandon the training
- redesign the training – new sequence, new methods, new content, new trainer
- redesign the preparation/pre-work – new briefing material, new pre-course work
- rethink the timing of the training – earlier or later in people's careers, earlier or later in the training programme, earlier or later in the company calendar
- leave well alone.

Figure 4 provides an overview of some key questions.

Figure 4

ELEMENTS OF EVALUATION

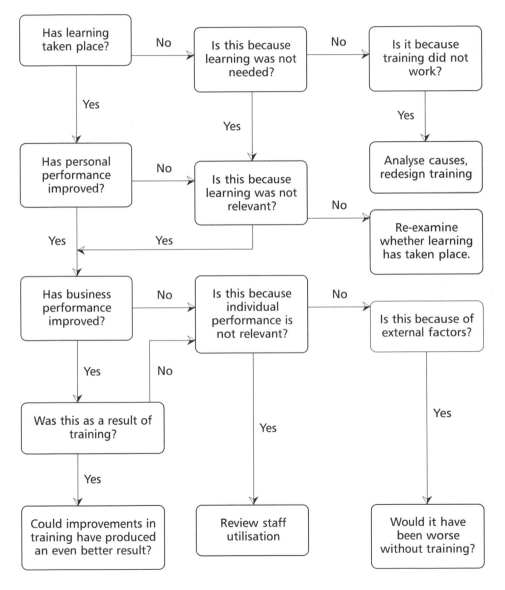

Approaches to evaluation

The most widely used approach dates back to the 1950s. It focuses on

1   the reactions of trainees – ie what they thought of the training
2   the learning that has taken place as a result of the training
3   changes which follow in behaviour in the job
4   the impact on results for the organisation.

Reactions level

Evaluation at this level typically takes the form of some sort of 'happy sheet'. This is a somewhat derisory reference to the fact that post-course questionnaires used to gauge reactions tend to paint a rosy picture of the event – often coloured by the quality of the food or the sociability of the delegates.

> Think back to any training course you have attended recently.
>
> Was there a post-course reactions questionnaire?
>
> If so, how useful do you think your comments were to the trainer?

The format ranges from the relatively simple – 'highlight the best and worst aspects' – to a detailed, session by session rating of tutor preparation, presentation, content, opportunities for participation and feedback, and so on. They may be designed specifically for each course or follow a general format. Computer software is now available to generate them automatically on the basis of pre-specified objectives.

Learning level

We saw in Chapter 4 how the objectives of particular

learning events may be focused on knowledge, skills, or attitudes. So evaluation may be directed at whichever of these is relevant to a particular learning activity.

Ways of testing whether knowledge has been acquired vary from formal, three-hour written papers, tackled unseen by the trainees and marked by internal or external examiners, to relatively short open-book tests, multiple choice objective tests, case-studies, interviews, quizzes, group exercises or self-reports.

Skills can be tested through observation by trained assessors or by trainees themselves, using role plays, simulations or real life tasks.

The assessment of changes in attitude is perhaps the most complex area, requiring the design of valid and reliable questionnaires and survey instruments. This is not a job for the novice.

Behaviour level

As we saw in Chapter 4, objectives which focus on the competencies needed in a job can draw together knowledge and skills and link them to the particular behaviour required. Again, there are many different ways of assessing whether the desired changes in behaviour have been mastered, and again the degree of formality varies.

Observation of the trainee at work or undertaking exercises, simulations and demonstrations may be one element. Formal rating of behaviour, by the trainee, their boss and their colleagues – as in the kind of 360° appraisal mentioned in Chapter 3 – may also have a part to play. Where the competencies are those required for the award of an NVQ, line managers or others trained as assessors, along with an external verifier, may do the assessment.

Results level

Assessing the impact of training on the effectiveness with which the organisation as a whole reaches its objectives is among the hardest, but most important, aspects of evaluation. The precise methods used will depend on the nature of the organisation's main goals and the factors it has identified as critical to its successful performance.

Questions may arise around issues such as whether there is any statistical correlation between, for instance, employee hours devoted to training, and profit, sales turnover, return on capital or other more immediate indicators of business performance such as the number of customer complaints, number of rejects, level of employee turnover and so forth.

Evaluation at this level could also entail collating the costs of training (see Chapter 2) and attempting to set these against the value of specific business improvements. In some cases this may be relatively straightforward. Suppose that, in order to pitch for a new contract worth $£x$ over one year, you recruited and then trained six new people – at a cost of $£y$ over one year. If x is greater than y, the training was probably worthwhile – depending on the other costs of servicing the contract.

Unfortunately in most businesses things are less clear-cut. Attributing a specific sales or profit gain solely to training can be very dubious. So many other internal factors – changes of systems, procedures, personnel and so on – and external factors – the economic climate, competitor activity, market trends etc – also have a bearing. That is why some of the other indicators mentioned above can be more useful. The problem then is to work out how much a 5 per cent reduction in customer complaints is actually worth, in the short and medium term. Although methods exist to do this, they usually have to be based on rather a lot of assumptions about customers' lifetime buying habits and the impact of complaints on their own and their acquaintances' buying behaviour.

At whatever level the evaluation is carried out, the tools used to do it must be both reliable – producing consistent results – and valid, measuring accurately whether or not objectives have been achieved.

Clearly the subject of evaluation is a large one. In Peter Bramley's *Evaluating Training* in this series, you will find more detailed examples of the kind of tools appropriate to evaluation at each level. Most can be applied before and during training, as well as after – in an attempt to measure the precise impact of the training and particular parts of it. There, too, you will find discussion of other types of evaluation – such as responsive evaluation – which focuses on the perceptions of key stakeholders about the effectiveness of the training. The important issue of the link between assessment or testing and evaluation is also addressed.

As you can see, the evaluation of training can be a major task, especially where large numbers of programmes, some internal, some external, some on-job, some off-job, are operating simultaneously. If it is taken seriously it can occupy a significant proportion of the trainer's time and call for yet another set of skills, over and above those so far identified.

Evaluation skills

You may need to

▮ design, administer or analyse questionnaires to gauge reactions to learning

▮ design, administer, invigilate or mark examinations

▮ arrange visits from external verifiers

▮ design, administer, observe or assess practical demonstrations of competency

▮ record, analyse and monitor trends in both reactions and test results to highlight actual or potential problems and assess implications for both trainees and trainers

▮ interview or use performance appraisal reports, individual performance results or other data to gauge impact on job performance. This may take the form of formal follow-up to the methods discussed in Chapter 3.

∎ research and analyse opinions and attitudes towards training in general and its specific impact on particular business objectives. Formal questionnaires, structured interviews or less formal soundings may all have their place.

∎ provide feedback to other trainers about the perceived impact of their contributions. This can be a particularly sensitive area. Sometimes trainers who perceive themselves as providing effective training have actually lost sight of the objectives or chosen methods they enjoy using, rather than those best calculated to help trainees learn. Identifying this may not be easy. Trainees may not readily recognise that the most enjoyable sessions are not necessarily the most productive. Reactions solicited immediately after the training will be coloured by a number of factors, including how good it felt. Only when you, and they, understand how 'feeling good' impacts on transfer back to the job can this count for much.

Evaluation and Investors in People

In some organisations, competence and impact on job performance and the business as a whole are monitored by exception. So rather than routinely having to establish that a link exists, you may find yourself defending a particular programme or event that has been called into question. In view of the time, effort and relative imprecision of setting up on-going evaluation of every activity, this can be a pragmatic solution.

It will not, however, be enough if your organisation wishes to gain recognition as an Investor in People (IIP). As we saw in Chapter 1, evaluation is a key area for those aspiring to the National Standard. They must be able to demonstrate that their training is not only properly planned and delivered but that each of the processes outlined in Table 13 is in place.

Table 13

INVESTORS IN PEOPLE INDICATORS FOR EVALUATION
(with effect from 1 February 1997)

Indicator	Typical evidence
4.1 The organisation evaluates the impact of training and development actions on knowledge, skills and attitude.	Post-course questionnaires; follow-up discussions between trainees and their managers; some form of written or practical test.
4.2 The organisation evaluates the impact of training and development actions on performance.	Performance reviews; team meetings; staff or customer surveys; monitoring of results against key performance indicators.
4.3 The organisation evaluates the contribution of training and development to the achievement of its goals and targets.	Evidence of top-level reviews of the impact of training on achieving business goals; examples of performance improvements linked to training and development.
4.4 Top management understands the broad costs and benefits of training and developing employees.	Evidence that the costs and benefits of training are measured in broad terms, and that top management assesses whether the organisation's commitment to training and development is worthwhile.
4.5 Action takes place to implement improvements to training and development identified as a result of evaluation.	Evidence that where the need for improvement is identified, steps are taken to modify the training.
4.6 Top management's continuing commitment to training and developing employees is demonstrated to all employees.	Newsletters, briefing notes, notice-boards and other internal communications highlighting how training has contributed to performance, plus evidence that commitment is sustained even in adverse trading conditions.

The precise methods through which this is achieved will depend on the organisation. In some, improvements in employee turnover, reduction in customer complaints, or other 'hard' measures are feasible. In others, external recognition of the standards achieved, based on 'benchmarking' the company's processes against best practice may be part of the answer.

If there is a clear vision, values and mission and a process in place to ensure all employees understand them, the IIP assessor will gauge the effectiveness of that process by interviewing a cross-section of employees to see if they understand what they mean for them. If there is a mechanism for planning to achieve business objectives – attracting more customers, servicing existing customers better, improving the quality of the product – the IIP assessor will look for evidence that specific learning has been geared to this end and that the link is understood.

He or she will also look at whether, and how often, senior management meet to plan and review the impact that training is having in the attainment of their goals and how high up their agenda training issues are. This may involve the assessor sitting in on management meetings, interviewing directors and employees and reviewing agendas, minutes and other relevant documents.

> How much evidence can your organisation produce to show that it meets the IIP standard for evaluation laid down in Table 13?

In addition, IIP assessors will take a particular interest in the mechanisms which exist to identify individual training needs and review the extent to which these have been met. Formal appraisal and review systems have their part to play here. So, too, do open systems of self-nomination for additional training.

If your organisation's employees are not yet among the five million or so now covered by the Standard, you may be involved in any or all of the activities identified in Table 14.

Table 14

ACTIVITIES INVOLVED FOR THE TRAINER IN THE JOURNEY TO IIP STATUS

Activity	Explanation
▮ Explaining the Standard and what is involved in achieving it	to ensure managers and employees at all levels understand what it entails and implies; your local TEC will be able to supply information packs, produced by Investors in People UK, and other help with briefing.
▮ Undertaking an initial informal review of your organisation's training processes	to help management decide whether, and when, to take matters further.
▮ Liaising with the local TEC	to set up an initial formal diagnosis with a trained adviser.
▮ Liaising with the adviser	to produce and implement an action plan to put in place any elements that the diagnosis reveals are lacking.
▮ Advising management	to make sure they understand the steps required and on the timing of the assessment.
▮ Providing background information	to provide a context for the assessment. You will need to supply information about the company, its ownership, history, structure, size, objectives, etc.
▮ Collating the documentary evidence in a portfolio to show that you have the necessary planning, implementation and review processes in place	to enable the assessor to judge how many of the indicators you can satisfy. The assessor will not be impressed by pious statements from the chief executive or expensive-looking off-job training programmes. Clear, concise, up-to-date records of actual training and follow-up, examples of changes made as a result of feedback received and formal certification of competence levels are far more likely to be persuasive. Your portfolio should be concise but comprehensive and indexed to show how specific documents relate to the 23 elements of the Standard.
▮ Arranging review meetings and interviews for the assessor	to ensure the assessor sees a representative sample. You cannot choose who gets involved – the assessor must be given free rein to identify how many and which employees should be available for individual or group meetings – and when.
▮ Supplying whatever other help the assessor requires	to make sure he or she has access to additional data, people, records and so on.
▮ Continuing to monitor and improve all your training and development systems and processes	even after your organisation has received recognition as an Investor in People, you will need to be ready for reassessment in three years' time.

If your organisation is already recognised, the challenge of continuous improvement to ensure you still meet the Standard when it is time for reassessment is considerable.

Roles and responsibilities

In some organisations it is assumed that each trainer will seek and act on feedback about reactions and learning. In others, evaluation is separated from actual delivery, to provide some measure of independent quality assurance.

In some, the trainees tend to be seen as 'the customer' and their feedback is a major influence. In others, line managers, the trainees' bosses, hold sway. Where evaluation is taken seriously, trainers, trainees, their bosses and senior management will all have a part to play.

The trainer

may focus on the process of training itself, and the extent to which

▎ reactions are positive
▎ test results indicate learning has taken place.

Line managers

will make observations on the impact on job performance, with the trainer encouraging a structured and objective approach to this. In instances where managers do not feel that training has helped, it will usually be for the trainer to work with the line manager to plan remedial action, rather than indulging in blame casting. It may be necessary to think back through the process of identifying needs, planning and delivering the training, and subsequent work situations to identify just where the problem stems from, what can be done to rectify it and to prevent repetition.

Senior managers

may seek the assistance of personnel specialists to monitor career progression, succession plans and employee turnover. On the basis of this, they will want to know how the training that is in place will impact on these indicators, in both the short and medium term. They will want to be satisfied that

▌ those who can contribute to the achievement of specific business objectives are being trained in a way that enables them to maximise their contribution

▌ all the training that is being conducted is good value for money.

External providers

if any have been involved, may appropriately be asked to provide some evaluation – at least at the reactions and learning levels. Alternatively, independent assessment may be useful.

IIP assessors

will not generally evaluate your training directly for you. Their task is to evaluate the processes you have in place to enable you to evaluate it yourself – to make sure your commitment to continue to deliver effective training to all your employees is sustainable. This transcends the question of whether a particular event met its objectives. Even if it didn't, the assessor – and the TEC recognition panel to whom he or she recommends the award – would be primarily concerned about whether you had identified the fact and taken remedial action.

In brief

I Evaluation is about trying to assess whether or not training is producing relevant and valued outputs through efficient and well-managed processes.

I It is itself a process – of gathering information with which to make decisions about training activities.

I Evaluation may be used for feedback, control, intervention.

I It can be carried out on reactions, learning, behaviour, results.

I Its focus may be the individual, the team or the organisation as a whole.

I Different tools for evaluation may be appropriate at different levels.

I The tools used include those listed in Table 15.

I Whichever tools are used must be both reliable – producing consistent results and valid – measuring accurately whether or not objectives have been achieved

I Some tools can be used before, during and after training, to measure progress

I The Investors in People Standard puts considerable emphasis on the importance of evaluation and defines six indicators of whether or not appropriate evaluation is taking place

I The conduct of evaluation is not a task for the trainer alone, but will involve trainees, their managers, colleagues, senior management and, sometimes, customers, suppliers, and external training providers.

Table 15

TOOLS FOR EVALUATION

Learning Tools	Reactions	Learning	Behaviour	Results
Delegate questionnaires or reports	∎	∎	∎	∎
Manager questionnaires or reports	∎	∎	∎	∎
Written test or examination		∎		
Practical test or demonstration		∎	∎	
Customer survey			∎	∎
Employee survey			∎	∎
Interviews	∎	∎	∎	∎
Performance appraisal		∎	∎	
Observation		∎	∎	
Company financial results				∎
Company results on other relevant performance indicators				∎
Results on team/departmental performance indicators				∎
Results on personal performance indicators				∎
Top management opinion	∎	∎	∎	∎
Recognition as Investor in People				∎

10 The Way Ahead

Introduction

The work of the trainer does not stand still. Within each of the aspects discussed in previous chapters and in the function as a whole, new government initiatives, advances in technology and management thinking and new research findings make sure of that.

In this final chapter we shall explore some of the trends which may influence the direction in which training continues to develop. In particular we shall consider:

I the concept of the learning organisation
I the trainer as coach versus the trainer as instructor
I the trainer as performance improvement consultant
I priorities for the twenty-first century
I future skills
I professional development.

The learning organisation

Some organisations stagger blindly from one crisis to the next, never pausing to draw out the lessons from one disaster before the next is upon them. Others consciously plan for and cope with change, and learn continuously from it. Those in the second category are examples of learning organisations.

> A learning organisation harnesses the full brainpower, knowledge and experience available to it, in order to evolve continually for the benefit of its stakeholders. (Andrew Mayo and Elizabeth Lank, *People Management*, 16 November 1995.)

Becoming a learning organisation is not something that happens by accident. It happens as a result of a conscious, strategic decision to create the kind of culture that supports learning, and to put in place the processes that will enable it to happen. There is no one formula – but a number of well-publicised variations on the same theme.

We touched in Chapter 3 on the link between training and business planning. In a learning organisation, business plans will be about learning. The chief executive, or other very senior champion, will see learning as being as much a part of what the organisation is about as the products it creates or the money it makes. Management style (see below), performance management and reward systems will all be geared to encouraging learning rather then maintaining the *status quo*.

The precise forms of learning that are embraced by learning organisations vary. Most will include a significant element of self-development, encouraged by the provision of diagnostic tools, opportunities to work with others who share the same objectives in a learning set or group, and ready access to technology-based and other learning resources. David Megginson and Vivien Whitaker describe in *Cultivating Self-development* how this works in practice.

Some organisations devote considerable resources simply to enable employees to develop the habit of learning. The Rover Learning Business, part of the Rover car group, is one example. It operates on the premiss that employees who are used to learning will make a greater contribution than those who have 'switched off their brains'. So even if the knowledge or skills to be learnt have no direct relevance to work, the company will still provide financial support.

Team learning, to enable those who work together to plan and learn together, is another important facet of the learning organisation. This recognises that the whole is usually greater than the sum of the parts and that teams that have shared goals, common experiences, and mutual understanding are stronger than collections of individuals, however bright.

Over and above this, the learning organisation will have in place the means of sharing learning across the business. This may take many forms, from formal feedback sessions from individuals who have attended external training events, to the development of databases of best practice and expertise. Particularly in large, decentralised organisations, networking – whether by computer or in person – is crucial in preventing wheels that have already been invented by one team being reinvented by others.

> What processes are in place in your organisation to share learning?

Learning organisations are the embodiment of many of the trends in training and learning which have evolved over the years. We shall explore some of the other key ones in the next sections.

The trainer as coach versus the trainer as instructor

As we saw in Chapter 1, the role of the trainer varies from organisation to organisation. One common thread which does seem to have emerged in recent years is the move

- away from didactic, classroom-based instruction in 'how to do it' (whether 'it' is threading a sewing machine or managing a department)
- towards much more emphasis on coaching to allow the learner to take responsibility and, with support and guidance, work out how 'it' works best for them. We explored this in Chapter 5.

Alongside this evolution in training styles, there has been an equally fundamental shift in training roles. As organisations become more complex and the pace of change gets faster, few can really pretend they know all the answers. Instead of trying to be ready with the solution to every problem, trainers have learnt what perhaps they always knew. By holding a mirror up to the questioner you can often find a better and more workable solution than proposing something from outside.

Management consultants have known this for years. There is an unkind saying that a consultant will 'borrow your watch and then tell you the time'. What it means is that outsiders rarely have an instant recipe to transform your business. Instead what they do is help you see the weaknesses in your present approach and identify some of the options you might choose to improve matters. Whether you do choose – and then whether you do everything necessary to make the chosen option work – is up to you.

This, increasingly, is what the trainer is attempting to do for the line manager. As line management's own responsibility for the development of their people has become clearer and more widely accepted, they have become less ready to off-load that responsibility on to a faceless collection of 'trainers' – whether internal or external.

This, in turn, is a response to some fundamental rethinking of the role of management. The old 'command and control', 'tell and direct' style of the traditional autocratic manager of the first half of the century was overtaken, in the 1960s, 1970s and 1980s, by the democratic, consensus-seeking manager. He or she still shared some of the fundamental beliefs of the traditionalists but sought to involve people more and take account of their ideas. By the late 1980s the democratic model was giving way to the much more rigorous and demanding philosophy of empowerment.

The empowering manager believes that every employee

∎ is capable of taking responsibility for his or her own actions

∎ can contribute more than traditional job descriptions allow

∎ is able to develop and grow.

They see their own role as that of coach and enabler, helping to co-ordinate the resources needed to allow their people to get the job done – and get it done better. If their people are not able to get the job done, the manager must do whatever is in his or her power to help. That includes coaching the team, coaching individuals, coaching suppliers, colleagues – anyone who, by behaving differently, can help.

> Is the prevailing style of management in your organisation autocratic, democratic or empowering? What examples can you think of?

The more interested that managers are in helping their people to excel, the more they will look to the trainer to ask them the questions that will enable them to focus on

∎ what they want their people to be able to do

∎ what resources are available, from within the team and elsewhere

∎ how they will know when they have achieved their goal.

In that context, what the line manager needs is someone who can, in turn, coach him or her. Someone who will help to identify and review alternatives – rather than someone who will provide the answers. This is a role many trainers are seeing as a way forward.

But in the truly empowered, learning organisation, it is recognised that neither trainers nor line managers should be the primary drivers of training. It is individuals themselves who have the primary responsibility to ensure that they get appropriate training and development at every stage in their careers. The ways in which they will do this are many and various and are discussed in detail in *Cultivating Self-development* by David Megginson and Vivien Whitaker.

Almost certainly they will include elements of self-paced, technology-based learning – and the other types of learner-centred learning we discussed in Chapter 5. Already more than 20 per cent of learning in America is acquired through technology and it is estimated that this will reach 50 per cent by the turn of the century. While formal courses may continue to have a role, this is likely to be much diminished.

As individuals choose, or are forced by job insecurity, to take on this responsibility, the implications for the trainer are profound. Unless they adapt their role they may find they have little contribution to make.

The trainer as performance improvement consultant

This is the label which is beginning to be applied to the future role of the professional trainer. It implies that supporting self-development and linking it to the achievement of improved business performance will be the way forward. The focus will be on forming and nurturing partnerships with line managers in order to help them appreciate the wider implications of improving performance.

In this context, options and solutions well beyond the scope of the conventional training plan will need to be embraced. The whole range of personnel policy and practice – from recruitment and reward to communications and career planning – will come into play. Organisation structures and the design of business processes will be as much part of the performance improvement consultant's thinking as the choice of learning methods or the design of training programmes. Project management and the management of change will take over from course management and presentation as their key skills. In so far as there continues to be a demand for the delivery of conventional training, most organisations will use external providers rather than employing in-house specialists.

This is not a flight of fancy. It is already reality in many organisations in the US – as delegates to a recent conference of the American Society of Training and Development confirmed. To help you prepare for this new and different perspective on your role, we shall focus briefly on some of the key elements.

Business transformation

Many managers have, for years, tried harder to do a good job while losing ground to competitors – particularly to the Japanese. What many have now realised is that 'trying harder' just is not the answer. In order to transform the performance of the organisation what is needed is a fundamental re-think of the way it works. The main steps in the process are to:

▌ look critically at the vision and mission of the company

▌ identify the critical success factors or things which must be achieved if the vision and mission are to be attained

▌ define which processes are central to the critical success factors – and what each is intended to achieve

▌ understand exactly how each core process works, using flow charts or models to capture the key activities and roles and responsibilities involved

▌ take detailed and repeated measurements to establish what each process is currently delivering and identify where and why delays and errors occur

▌ use systematic problem-solving techniques to tackle the causes of failure

▌ re-engineer the processes to avoid unnecessary inspection, movement, delays and duplication

■ build in fail-safes to prevent errors and defects

■ re-define roles and responsibilities and train people to use the revised processes

■ put new measures in place and monitor performance.

Central to this model of business transformation is an approach known as business process re-engineering (BPR). Apart from a stringent and very systematic method of approach, one of the things that sets BPR apart is the emphasis on processes.

> Business processes are the sequences of tasks through which an organisation converts 'inputs' into 'outputs' for its customers. The inputs will include ideas, knowledge, skill, cash and physical resources. The outputs may be anything from a comfortable night's sleep – if you are in the hotel trade – to a carrier bag full of groceries – if you are in food retailing – to an attractive and secure home – if you are in domestic house building.
>
> The processes are the threads running through the business. They are the channels along which effort, materials, information and other resources flow.
>
> If processes are well designed and functioning, they will ensure your customers' wants are met. If they are not, everyone in the organisation will spend a disproportionate amount of time disentangling them.

Another of the key characteristics of BPR is its reliance on teams. By definition, most of the processes that really make a difference to whether the business achieves its mission (its core processes) span a number of the specialist functions that make up the business.

In a hotel, for example, the laundering of dirty linen, the provision of courtesy refreshments and the replacement of defective light bulbs would, in some establishments, be the responsibility of different departments. But if the guest is to find a properly equipped room on arrival, the process through which these things are brought together must work smoothly. Any gaps, bottlenecks or duplication of effort are most likely to be identified by getting the laundry staff, the provisions staff and the servicing staff together to decide what can be done to enhance the comfort of their guests.

Such a cross-functional team approach brings together a range of knowledge and skills relating to current practice and ideas about what can be done to improve it. If the team is then empowered to take the action necessary to streamline the process, the customer should see a real change for the better.

Process improvement

Organisations that do not see the need for total transformation may nevertheless have plenty of scope for improving the way they do things. A whole raft of techniques can be brought to bear to make sure that every one of the processes that your organisation operates is as effective and as efficient as possible.

> List the processes in which you work. Who is your 'customer' and how well does the process serve them? How is this measured, and by whom?

Flowcharting and systematic problem-solving, control charts, Pareto and other statistical techniques all form part of the repertoire of those engaged in process improvement. You will find information about what they involve and how to use them in Tom Boydell and Malcolm Leary's *Identifying Training Needs*.

The performance improvement consultant's role

Tasks for the performance improvement consultant will include

▌ advising on the speed and direction of process improvement or transformation projects and encouraging prompt and effective decision-making at key points

▌ acting as team facilitator, coaching the cross-functional teams and their leaders in the use of the diagnostic, problem-solving, measurement and decision-making tools appropriate at each stage

▌ helping the teams to identify individual and team training needs and ways of using the resources of the team to meet them. People who have been used to working as individuals do not always adjust immediately to become effective team workers. Those skilled in team-building can find themselves much in demand as new teams form and try to get established

▌ documenting and recording new processes so the team will not to revert to the old way of doing things.

Priorities for the twenty-first century

Empowerment and business process re-engineering are both issues of the 1990s. Both seem, in today's climate of change, to have within them the seeds of an enduring new approach to the way people work. Wider social and political forces make it unlikely that we shall revert to the old narrow definitions of individual jobs with narrow bands of skills taught by specialist trainers.

So one priority for trainers in the next century will be to continue to develop their skills as coaches and consultants; facilitators who can get the best out of teams and foster individual learning. Over and above this there are three other trends that are likely to impact on trainers and how they operate.

Technology

Virtual reality, the Internet and the Information Super-Highway are no longer science fiction. Bill Gates, head of

Microsoft, the world's leading software company, predicts a revolution in the amount and quality of information to which we shall all soon have access. For the trainer this is both a threat and an opportunity.

A threat – because, as we have seen, the days of straight information-giving in standard presentation format could be numbered. It will be quicker, cheaper and more fun to get it from our screens. An opportunity – because all this knowledge has to come from somewhere. Knowledge which is unique or confidential to the company must be originated and presented from within the company – in a format accessible and appealing to those who work there. For the trainer whose expertise lies in constructing concepts so others can grasp them, the Information Super-Highway is just a much more exciting, dynamic and interactive training vehicle.

Language and culture

More and more organisations now see the world as their market place, their source – or both. Helping people learn other languages may or may not a be a job for the in-company trainer – but helping them adjust to new cultures and ways of living could be. More businesses are beginning to realise how ineffective it is to send people off around the world with a smattering of the language and none of the culture. Few go so far as to post out 'cultural trainers' to help, relying instead on local agents or other managers to do the job. Depending on what is at stake, deploying the skills of the trainer to expedite learning can pay dividends – as it often does for inward investors into Britain.

The environment

Patterns of work are already changing. As more employees work from home via computer networks, the trainer will need to find ways of helping them to learn that do not involve travel to central courses. Technology-based training is again likely to be the main growth area.

Future skills

The exact requirements of the trainer of the future will depend on the industry, the employer and the level and nature of the role. In some, administration and record-keeping will continue to have a high profile. In others, interpersonal skills will be critical. In yet others, the ability to assist learning through the development of text and graphics will be more important.

As we have seen, the emphasis is likely to be on helping people – and organisations – to learn, rather than traditional trainer input.

The check-list in Table 16 should be seen as a list of possibilities rather than a definitive prescription.

Table 16

TRAINER SKILLS

Skill	Application
Interpersonal skills	to establish rapport at all levels; questioning, listening and summarising are crucial.
Analytical and evaluative skills	for interpreting behaviour and information, including financial and other numerical data.
Communication skills	to convey new and challenging ideas clearly, logically and succinctly.
Creative skills	to design imaginative approaches to communication and training.
Administrative skills	to ensure training is planned, recorded and monitored effectively.
Commercial awareness	to ensure training resources are used cost-effectively and, in some instances, profitably – to serve the needs of the business.
Technical skills	to operate computer systems and, possibly, develop technology-based training modules.
Personal credibility	as someone who knows about, and can add value to, the learning process.

continued on page 164

Table 16 (continued)

TRAINER SKILLS

Skill	Application
Wide knowledge and understanding of the organisation, its goals, values and processes	to contribute to the re-engineering of business processes and to develop learning which is consistent with corporate goals and values.
Integrity	to safeguard the confidentiality of information. Trainers are increasingly involved in sensitive personal and business issues.
Respect for authority	to help establish the norms of the organisation. You need to be accepted as part of its management team.
Tolerance of ambiguity	as organisations and individuals struggle with new learning challenges, trainers will often find themselves pulled in different directions.

Professional development

The professional body for those involved in training is the Institute of Personnel and Development (IPD). There are seven grades of membership:

■ affiliate – no study required

■ associate – achieved through meeting standards in one area

■ licentiate – achieved through meeting standards in one field

■ graduate – achieved through meeting standards in three fields

■ member – three years' relevant experience and approved continuing professional development (CPD)

■ fellow – 10 years' relevant experience and approved CPD

■ companion – significant contribution to profession: bestowed by invitation only.

There are five possible routes into membership:

■ educational through an IPD approved course of study

■ competence assessment against national standards (NVQ/SVQ)

■ professional assessment against IPD standards

■ assessment of prior certificated learning through an approved IPD alternative qualification or individual assessment

■ a combination of the above.

As a training professional, you will need to think in terms of attaining graduate membership at least. Unless you already have an NVQ in training and development or management you will need to approach one of the Institute's 400 approved centres, nationwide. These include universities, colleges of further and higher education, training consultancies and commercial organisations; the IPD Professional Education Department can send you a full list. You can then choose whether to follow a specialist training and development route – after completing core modules on general management and personnel and development – or follow a more generalist personnel route.

Obtaining graduate membership is only the first step. Like many other professions, the IPD recognises that knowledge and skills quickly become out-dated and are in need of constant renewal. Underpinned by the concept of life-long learning, the Institute's policy of continuing professional development (CPD) emphasises each individual's responsibility for his or her own learning. There are three main requirements:

■ Members are expected to structure their learning and keep a record of it.

■ Evidence of CPD must be provided to support applications to upgrade membership.

■ All corporate members are required to undertake CPD and may be asked to participate in random surveys.

A wide range of different activities can contribute towards CPD – from attendance at branch events, seminars and conferences to self-development activities, coaching and mentoring. While some professional bodies insist on specifying a set number of hours or attendance at specific training events, the IPD has chosen to rely on its members to structure development to meet personal needs, recording the outcomes in a personal learning-log. A CPD pack, including a record sheet, development plan and computer disk for charting and planning development is issued free to members.

For further information about CPD, and for details of both the professional education scheme and the programme of short courses offered by the Institute you can contact them at the address on page iv.

In brief

- The development of learning organisations, working to harness the brainpower, knowledge and experience of their people, reflects the fundamental importance of training and learning for those organisations that hope to prosper in the next millennium.
- The trend towards a more 'empowering' style of management and an increasing emphasis on self-development have combined to bring about a move
  - ☐ away from didactic instruction towards coaching and facilitation
  - ☐ away from 'trainer' towards 'performance improvement consultant'.
- Organisations are increasingly recognising the importance of a process view of the business.
- Many have embarked on wholesale business process re-engineering; others are focused on process improvement.
- All need a range of diagnostic, measurement, problem-solving and design tools which were not part of the traditional trainer's repertoire.

∎ These trends are likely to continue into the next decade, and we are likely also to see

  ☐ increased use of virtual reality, the Internet and multi-media training

  ☐ emphasis on cross-cultural development

  ☐ remote learning to reflect changing patterns of work.

∎ The skills the trainer will need will depend on the particular role, but in so far as it is possible to generalise we attempted to do so in Table 16.

∎ Membership of the IPD, via one of their five routes of entry, is a key step for professional trainers. Continuing professional development is a life-long commitment.

11 Further Reading and Advice

Books

Your starting-point for delving deeper into many of the topics discussed in the preceding chapters will be the other books in the IPD's *Training Essentials* series. They are:

- *Cultivating Self-development*, David Megginson and Vivien Whitaker
- *Delivering Training*, Suzy Siddons
- *Designing Training*, Alison Hardingham
- *Developing Learning Materials*, Jacqui Gough
- *Evaluating Training*, Peter Bramley
- *Identifying Training Needs*, Tom Boydell and Malcolm Leary.

One of the most thorough general texts in this field is *Employee Development* by Rosemary Harrison (in the *People and Organisations* series), London, IPD 1997.

To understand more about learning theory and learning styles, consult *The Manual of Learning Styles* by Peter Honey and Alan Mumford, third edition, Honey, 1992; *Understanding How People Learn* by D. Reay, London, Kogan Page, 1994; and *Experiential Learning* by D.A. Kolb, Englewood Cliffs, NJ, Prentice Hall, 1984.

For guidance on identifying relevant competencies, see *Competencies in Action* by Jane Weightman, London, IPD, 1994, which gives a thorough and up-to-date overview.

For further examples consult the *MCI Pocket Directory, Middle Management Standards*, London, the Management Charter Initiative.

The key work on organisational core competencies is 'The core competence of the corporation', by Gary Hamel and C.K. Prahalad, *Harvard Business Review*, 1990.

For specific advice on performance appraisal consult *Appraisal: Routes to improved performance* by Clive Fletcher, London, IPD, 1993 and *The Appraisal Discussion* (in the *Training Extras* series) by Terry Gillen, London, IPD, 1995.

You will find valuable guidance on designing and using development centres in *Assessment Centres: Identifying and developing competence* by Charles Woodruffe, second edition, London, IPD, 1994.

For defining learning objectives, the standard text is probably still that by R. F. Mager, which is simply called *Preparing Instructional Objectives*, published by Fearon Publishers in 1961.

For a clear and comprehensive guide to coaching using the Goal, Reality, Options, Will (GROW) model outlined in Chapter 5, consult: *Coaching to Improve Performance* by John Whitmore, London, Nicholas Brealey, 1992. A useful, concise guide is provided by Eric Parsloe's *The Manager as Coach and Mentor* (in the *Training Extras* series), published by the IPD, London, 1995.

For specific guidance on designing an induction programme, try *Employee Induction: A good start* by Alan Fowler, third edition, London, IPD, 1996.

When it comes to tracking down role plays and exercises, there are a number of well-established collections. The best of these make the objectives of each exercise and the target audience clear, and include detailed advice on administration and debriefing – for example, the long-established handbooks and annuals by Pfeiffer and Jones, published by University Associates Publishers and Consultants, San Diego; or try *Adair's Management Development Exercises* by John Adair and Terry Gillen, London, IPD, 1997.

For guidance on how to compare internal and external providers try *Management Development: Strategies for action* by Alan Mumford, second edition, London, IPD, 1993.

For general advice on using consultants, a good starting-point is *Using the HR Consultant* by Michael Armstrong, London, IPD, 1994. Follow this by referring to a directory such as *The Directory of Assessment and Development Consultants*, Executive Grapevine Volume 5, 1995/6.

To help you choose a consultant for a specific assignment, contact the IPD Personnel Consultancy Assignment Service. They will offer you access to the professional expertise of IPD member consultants. Your local TEC also keeps a register of approved consultants.

Training directories

These are an invaluable first port of call when you need to track down possible suppliers. *The National Training Index* and *Omtrac* are among the best known, while Hewlett Packard's *On Demand: Information multimedia network for training and personnel professionals* is a more recent alternative. Your local TEC also has access both to national and local databases.

Individual providers advertise in trade and professional journals as well as targeting mailshots to companies they think may be interested in their services. The larger ones, colleges, and business schools produce a full programme with regular updates. These, too, are available on request.

Further and Higher Education

Course guides and individual prospectuses can give an indication of the sort of specialisms on offer at particular institutions. Staff may take on consultancy work on behalf of the school, or privately. Some have a short-course brochure available on request giving details of open courses and an indication of the scope for tailoring.

Technology-based materials

Individual providers will send you their catalogues on request.

Courses

In addition to the IPD's professional programme (see Chapter 10) and its programme of short courses, a number of other bodies offer relevant training. For example, GBS (Guardian Business Services) Training offer a three-day course on identifying training needs, plus other specialist modules. Their address is 75 Farringdon Road, London EC1M 3JB.

Sundridge Park, Bromley, Kent provides short courses on the use of technology-based training. Performance Consultants offer open or dedicated coaching programmes using the GROW model. Their address is Suite 500, 150 Regent Street, London W1R 5FA.

To establish which local providers may be able to support external elements of a particular programme, and to find out more about Modern Apprenticeships, Youth Training and other Government initiatives, talk to your local TEC. They, or your employers' association or federation if you belong to one, can also advise on relevant qualification links – or you can discuss these direct with the awarding bodies.

Index